A HISTORY OF COUNTY GALWAY

A HISTORY OF COUNTY
Galway

Peadar O'Dowd

GILL & MACMILLAN

Gill & Macmillan Ltd
Hume Avenue, Park West, Dublin 12
with associated companies throughout the world
www.gillmacmillan.ie

© Peadar O'Dowd 2004

0 7171 3687 6
Index compiled by Helen Litton
Design by Graham Thew Design
Print origination by Carrigboy Typesetting Services, Co. Cork
Printed by ColourBooks Ltd, Dublin

This book is typeset in 11pt Post-Mediaeval on 14pt.

*The paper used in this book comes from the wood pulp of managed forests. For every tree felled,
at least one tree is planted, thereby renewing natural resources.*

A CIP catalogue record for this book is available from the British Library.

1   3   5   4   2

Cover photographs
(*clockwise from left*)
Kilmacduagh monastic site; Turoe Stone; Robert O'Hara Burke plaque;
seventeenth-century map of Galway town; Corrib estuary, 1820.

CONTENTS

I NATURAL FORMATION

NATURE CALLS

'**A**S OLD AS T*h*e HILLS' IS an apt expression when one looks at the physical entity that is County Galway today. The term implies natural antiquity and thanks to radiometric and fossil-dating techniques, we now have the means of finding out how ancient this Galway countryside is in the vast geological scale of time itself.

While older stones (one nearly said 'bones') have been discovered in faraway Wexford and nearby Mayo, the great mountain heart of Connemara, the Twelve Bens, in the western section of County Galway, began to form nearly seven hundred million years ago, as far back as we would like to go.

MOVING PLATES

Back then, the slow moving plates of the earth's crust re-created oceans and land masses in a confusing melody of change set in motion over a timescale of millions of years. The Atlantic Ocean had yet to form, and in its place an earlier ocean called Japetus separated what is now North

America, which was then joined to the north-west portion of Europe, from the rest of Europe itself.

Ireland, of course, had to be different. Put simply, the northern half lay in the North American section, while that portion lying south of a line from the Shannon to Dundalk lay in Europe. Thus, the beginnings of Connemara lay in the former section, its sedimentary rock formation dating to the Dalradian of the late Cambrian period laid down during the formation of the Japetus Ocean. As ever, beneath the earth's mantle the molten interior was restless and in time the basic rock called gabbro forced itself upwards forming a thick layer in the sedimentary foundations of this proto-Connemara. More gigantic changes were to follow.

The two continents were in motion, and slowly moving towards one another, the Japetus Ocean was squeezed dry by the new land formations, with the result that the Connemara rock foundations were folded and faulted as the continents collided. The two halves of Ireland were joined together and Connemara had found a permanent home about 450 million years ago as it slid into position over the volcanic rocks of Europe.

TWELVE BENS OF CONNEMARA

The metamorphic or changing effects on the basic rock formations of Connemara were immense. As well as the folding and faulting, a vast sandstone layer was metamorphosed into pure quartzite, clay into schists, and proto-limestones into the familiar green marble synonymous with Connemara today.

In time, a new moulder of the landscape comes into play. Years are now counted in the millions as weather spreads its relentless cloak of erosion to test these ancient rocklands. Sun, rain and ice are the main ingredients that carve their varied scripts on the Connemara landscape, as the softer schists weather away to lower elevations. Thus, the massive quartzite entity is left to thrust twelve massive elbows of grey, glittery peaks to meet the western skies. Called na Beanna Beola (the Twelve Bens), they are the flag-poles over the ancient heart of Connemara, with Binn Bhán at 730 m, the highest and proudest of them all.

They are not alone, of course, because across the Inagh Valley with its dark-watered Inagh and Derryclare lakes, rises yet another quartzite range delighting to the name of the Maam Turk mountains. Although they are not as high as their Ben sisters, they, too, run roughly in an east-west direction, with Binn Idir an Dá Log their highest point at 703 m, before the Maam Valley, where so much of the famous film, *The Quiet Man*, was shot in 1951, puts a halt to their eastward thrust.

METAMORPHIC CHANGES

Sufficient to say that the amazing mix of the quartzite peaks of the Bens and Turks right down to lake level, where green Connemara marble caresses the little hamlet of Recess, raises pulse rates among visiting geologists. Equally exciting are the endless glints of schists, while cloudy garnets near Cleggan and jasper outpourings along the shoreline at Lough Nafooey indicate the rich geological heritage of these western highlands of County Galway.

These semi-precious stones suggest much metamorphic and volcanic activity in the distant past, especially jasper, because more than one phase in the formation of this rock is evident on the Lough Nafooey landscape separating North Galway from South Mayo. While red jasper is found here, denoting a slower cooling of the lava on the earth's surface at this point, clusters of the green variety also occur, evidence of a swifter underwater formation process when these lands were submerged underneath an ocean as primeval as time itself.

GALWAY GRANITE

Even now, we are not finished with the gigantic changes wrought by nature, because 400 million years ago the earth was restless again and intruded its volcanic anger, this time across the southern flanks of Connemara verging on Galway Bay. Consequently, the dotted mounds of ruddy outcrops contain the appropriately named Galway Granite, a stone much sought after in modern times in its finished and finely polished form of pillar, pedestal and memorial plaque. Happily, there is life still in this igneous rock, for its pleasing mix of feldspar, mica and quartz lends a delightful colour combination to the polishing process, and the end result can be seen in stout, rounded pillars of gleaming granite in a number of Galway City churches.

While one could delve much deeper into the major geological periods and processes associated with the shaping of these fascinating highlands, it's time now to leave Connemara, a geologist's paradise, and travelling eastwards across the vast, dividing waters of Lough Corrib, we find the county stretching for over 60 km more, its limestone base formed in geological slumber.

LIMESTONE FORMATION

Not here, the upheavals of spewing magma and crushing plates, but rising seas during the Carboniferous Period of 300 million years ago brought new geological changes still evident in this section of East Galway, twice as large again as its rugged western appendage.

As Ireland sank into a warm, shallow, marine environment, the land, now the sea floor, was colonised by marine animals and plants, whose decaying bodies produced the mineral calcium carbonate so prevalent in the grass-covered limestone plains of East Galway. Big-boned animals, known simply as Galway Sheep, are proof positive of the natural endowment of these grasslands, which took place aeons ago.

GLACIAL TIMES

In more recent times, if one can describe two million years ago in such a way, nature was angry yet again and sent glacial fingers to greet a land recovering from a watery grave. The last great Ice Age had arrived, and with it new moulding forces changed the Galway landscape in ways familiar to the modern eye, not least the creation of two vast limestone basins, later to overflow from incessant rains and form Lough Corrib.

The massive Inagh Valley, its mountain sides made smooth by a third glacial movement known as the Connemara Phase, and nearby Killary Harbour, Ireland's only fjord, are other examples of Ice Age moulding in its final phases along fault lines already there. Here, one senses the powerful thrust of ancient glaciers when snow and frost mingled to form a mighty ice sheet, whose relentless grating movement towards the sea acted as a giant gouge or chisel that only nature could employ.

The residue scooped up by these glaciers, huge boulders of the afore-mentioned Galway Granite, were carried like confetti and deposited as erratics on the shorelines of Galway Bay or as underwater hazards in Lough Corrib. These immense boulders manifest the translating strength of the ancient ice flows, as do the great whales of sand and rolled pebbles that we know today as drumlins, rising high as grassy hillocks over bog and sea. Yet another contribution from the Gaelic language, the term originates in the word 'druim' (a ridge), denoting a streamlined mound of glacial drift. A prime example is Gentian Hill, which dominates Silver Strand, one of Galway City's famous seaside resorts on its western outskirts.

ESKERS

Inland, even more powerful glaciers created eskers, meandering ridges of sand and gravel formed by melt waters flowing as rivers beneath the ice sheets. Today, these high, sandy monuments to our glacial past vein eastern parts of County Galway in particular, with the more famous Eiscir Riada reaching its maritime destination near the water tower outside the village of Clarinbridge.

In the past, these eskers helped divide kingdoms, as did the Eiscir Riada when it divided Ireland into Leath Mogha and Leath Cuinn during Celtic times. Meanwhile, in the heart of the eastern section of County Galway, from Athenry to the famous Turoe Stone near Loughrea, use may have been made in Celtic times of these natural formations as defence features, but they had other potentials also.

Not generally noted was the fact that eskers were also ideal communication corridors set high above the canopy of endless forests, allowing a warring clan or humble saint alike to move more easily across the sea of green. In this regard the Eiscir Riada was also known as the Slí Mór (the Big Way), and despite some meanderings, one could depart from the seashore at Clarinbridge in these ancient times and travel with a little more facility to the east coast.

GORTIAN PERIOD

Yet even in this last great Ice Age, warm periods also occurred, and one in particular had a special Galway connection. Ancient sediments of over 50,000 years ago from the Gort area in South Galway best illustrate these changing climatic conditions. Here, pollen analyses record stunted plant growth giving way to the vibrant spread of ash, hazel and even oak, before grasses again herald the return of colder climes and the demise of these primeval woodlands. Consequently, this warm hiatus is called the Gortian Period and a small Galway town gives its name to an important period in Irish glacial history.

FAUNA

Fauna, too, appeared during these narrow warm bands, none more so than woolly mammoths and giant Irish deer with antlers to match. Red deer, wolves and even brown bears inhabited this emerging land also, but we have to wait until the actual ending of the last cold spell, some 12,000 years ago, before Ireland finally freed itself from retreating ice sheets.

As the landscape lost its white, silver hue, a welcome mat of green and blue awaited the arrival of man sometime after 8000 BC.

EARLY VEGETATION

Two thousand years before, a mixed tundra of rough grassland, heath and dwarf trees such as birch, fed by the new and warmer rains, gained a foothold on these emerging lands. The birch grew stronger and ever higher, competing now with hazel as the greening of Ireland began.

In time, giant forests of oak and pine greeted the first human arrivals, simple hunting and fishing folk who found perhaps more sustenance in the waters than the wild.

LAKE *and* RIVER FORMATION

Shellfish lay abundant by the seashores, while the emerging rivers were also kind. The estuaries were filled with mullet and bass, but the rivers were something else, and the River Corrib better than most. A short river of only 5 km, it helped shed the accumulating waters of its creator, Lough Corrib, only then slowly evolving into the largest lake in the Irish Republic. In time it would grow to 44,000 acres of clear blue water, filling first the great deep basin gouged or even faulted in earlier times between the angling centres of Oughterard and Headford.

The overflow moved south, at first as a small meandering river which began to fill another smaller, shallow basin below the present village of Annaghdown. The Lower Lake, snuggling into its nutrient-rich limestone base, slowly formed, and fed with new rivers from the east, overflowed its south-western boundary to form the River Corrib, the lake's final surge to Galway Bay. The third segment of the County Galway landscape, Lough Corrib, was complete.

GALWAY BAY

The forth had been formed when Galway Bay, according to the Irish Annals, was initially a lake known as Loch Lurgan, one of three noted in ancient Ireland. A high barrier reef kept the ocean at bay until the Atlantic finally burst through, leaving the Aran Islands as lonely sentinels of the former ocean baulk 'too high to be overflown by the billows'!

Today, shore walkers from Salthill to Spiddal point to remnants of 'bog oaks' and even portions of ancient bogs lying beneath the sands of present-day beaches all along the northern fringes of Galway Bay as proof that this catastrophic event actually took place.

SALMON *and* EEL

Meanwhile, the River Corrib would later change its course and depth, growing ever deeper and wider while rain patterns increased as time progressed. Not surprisingly, its outflow into Galway Bay left a signature new homing fish stocks simply could not ignore. Thus, began the wonderful friendship between Atlantic salmon and the humble eel with this great waterway, a friendship that lasts to the present day.

The amazing sight of hundreds of summer salmon or grilse at rest beneath the Salmon Weir Bridge in the heart of Galway City and the wide-scale netting of the silver eel there during dark nights in November confirm this natural wedding of humble fish and mighty waterway.

PEOPLE POWER

Perhaps the first people to arrive at the River Corrib estuary joined in the initial celebrations! Their descendants have done so ever since, and have provided the final moulding influence on the Galway landscape.

From initial simple land-clearing carried out by the newly arrived Neolithic or first farming people c. 4000 BC right down to present large-scale agricultural operations, the countryside has changed immeasurably, some might say for the worst. With vast road networking and town expansions, ribbon developments and water pollution increasing year by year, one wonders what the quality of our natural landscape will be in the future.

The CALL Of NATURE

All is not lost, however, because the call of nature is too strong to be ignored by the European Union right down to Galway County Council level. Already at local level, 'once-off housing' restrictions on farm land is coming into play, while local authorities are planning to produce water quality of the highest standard and quantity for a future world where water will be a far more precious commodity than it is today.

Proper planning, of course, was always the key to material success. From the simple land-clearing plans of early farmers in the Menlo area or of their peers on the western seaboard around Clifden, the human mind has moulded the landscape in two distinct ways.

HUMAN INFLUENCES

From clearing native oak and pine forests in Neolithic times to planting vast swathes of coniferous pine today along Connemara mountain and hill sides, or even the draining of the county's eastern bogs and rivers in land reclamation projects, the human mind has been active in planning specifically to move from mere subsistence to adding luxury to people's lives.

Land was the key to existence. As well as working it, acquiring it in the first place demanded planning of the highest order, as well as valour in the actual acquisition process. The might of the sword obviously came into the equation, but the universal constant for success was good planning, not only with a view to winning battles and gaining land, but in holding on to it afterwards.

ANCIENT TERRITORIES

Marking out territories became a necessity of ancient life from the Celtic era right down to Tudor times. Gradually, tuatha (petty kingdoms) merged under the might of overlords, with the O'Flahertys, for instance, becoming vassals of the O'Connors, kings of Connacht and, at times, monarchs of Ireland (with opposition).

With the arrival of the Anglo-Norman invaders in Galway in the thirteenth century under de Burgo lordships, these ancient Celtic territories were parcelled out to ensure that the chief de Burgo cabot at Loughrea was as safe as possible from the anger of the dispossessed.

The de Berminghams provided a northern arc of protection from O'Connor attack using their castles at Athenry, Dunmore and Moylough as defensive as well as offensive bases, while to the south the Fitzgeralds countered O'Brien incursions from their new base at Ardrahan, finally vacated by a disgruntled and quickly declining O'Heyne clan. However, the finest example of acquisition planning was the establishment of County Galway itself.

The MAKING Of COUNTY GALWAY

The year was 1584 when, for more efficient administration as well as military expediency, Sir John Perrot, Lord Deputy of Ireland, divided Connacht into six counties, including Clare which reverted back to Munster in 1602. County Galway then came into being, its territory based mainly on the old MacWilliam Uachtar possessions, but with more than a little help from nature in defining its actual boundaries.

In all, some 2,293 sq. miles were involved, with the ancient water-filled fault lines of Killary Harbour to the north and Galway Bay to the south as well as the Atlantic Ocean delineating its western boundary. The Rivers Suck and Shannon clearly indicated the eastern extremity, while the Aughty Mountains to the south and the Party Mountains as well as the northern edges of Lough Corrib sealed the county boundary lines in stone and water.

While some minor alterations were engendered in the nineteenth century when Inishboffin seceded from County Mayo and came to fly the county colours of maroon and white, Galway had already become the second largest county in Ireland, second only to Cork in size, but never in awe. Its story follows.

2 ANCIENT GALWAY

ANTIQUITY

'**A**NTIQUITY', **A WORD BATHED** in the past, raises more than usual interest because inherent in it is the mystery of human life lost in time itself. In the vast timescale of European civilisation, however, Irish antiquity verges on the present. While Neanderthals and Cro-Magnonians roamed ancient Europe for tens of thousands of years, it was only about 10,000 years ago as the post Ice Age Irish tundras changed to dense inland forests that human feet first tread along Irish coastlines and river banks.

EUROPE'S YOUNGEST RACE

The Irish, then, are one of Europe's youngest races, less than ten millenniums in existence. Our first inhabitants, Mesolithic or Middle Stone Age food gatherers, foraged ever further westwards for food from Britain. Perhaps in their wanderings they crossed a natural land bridge to Ireland, an eroding Ice Age moraine remnant by 8000 BC.

Shellfish, birds' eggs, fish and edible seaweeds helped complete their rudimentary diet as the setting western sun offered better pickings on the morrow. So intent were these nomadic groups on gathering food along these ancient shorelines that a new territory looming on the horizon may not have been noticed as they left their homeland behind.

When dense forests formed a vast impenetrable barrier to the interior for these nomads, they made their way around the coastlines, only foraging inland along river shorelines. Fishing and hunting with stone-tipped wooden implements augmented their food-gathering activities as they spread through an island very different from today.

GALWAY'S FIRST ARRIVALS

When the descendants of these initial Mesolithic peoples reached the estuary of the River Corrib about 6000 BC, salmon and eel stocks filled their hungry gaze. Not surprisingly, the flash of stone-tipped leisters said it all, and the satisfying smell of cooking has permeated Corrib banks ever since. Recent finds of chert and flint stone blades on ancient sub-merged river shorelines provide evidence of Galway City's first inhabitants, who may even have set up temporary homes beside the Corrib.

By 4000 BC, newcomers began to make County Galway their permanent home. Neolithic or New Stone Age people were our first farmers, and their primitive stone axes are found in many places in the county and especially on the bed of the River Corrib where ancient river banks were subsequently submerged by increasing water levels. Used to cut back the forest floor, these primitive farming implements indicate initial crop cultivation on cleared sites as well as animal husbandry in the Menlo region on the northern outskirts of Galway City.

While their humble wood and thatched homes have long since disappeared, a more permanent funerary monument is evident in the remnants of a portal dolmen in the nearby townland of Angliham on the shores of Lough Corrib. Only the two portal entry stones and one side stone of this megalithic tomb stand *in situ*, but the collapsed capstone and other debris of this stone building dedicated to the dead are all that remain of this ancient monument, dating perhaps to c. 3500 BC–the first entry in Galway City's built heritage.

STONE AGE COUSINS

Elsewhere in the county there is more archaeological evidence of the arrival and settlement of Stone Age farmers, especially along the north-west coastline between Clifden and Cleggan. Here, over thirty megalithic tombs of the court, portal and wedge types indicate the largest Neolithic settlement in the county, with recently identified pre-bog field walls there confirming a mostly pastoral-based farming economy.

This is verified by pollen diagrams from tiny Lough Sheeauns near Cleggan, which illustrate this initial human interplay with the natural landscape, before a loss of soil fertility, perhaps due to over-grazing, sees a population decline during the subsequent Bronze Age period in Ireland.

NATURE AGAIN TO The FORE

Despite these initial environment-changing efforts by man, nature was not quite finished with moulding the landscape. Rising sea levels may well have submerged Neolithic activities in South Connemara, while the varied placement of kitchen middens (ancient human refuse collections of burnt stone, shell mounds and charcoal spreads), especially in the Ballyconneely area and in the aforementioned Gentian Hill in Galway City, suggest sea movements still in vogue.

These, of course, would not have impacted on inland Neolithic settlements, where megalithic tombs beyond the eastern shores of Galway Bay around the Sliabh Aughty Mountains in South Galway and some outliers east of the Clare River and in North Galway near Glenamaddy indicate a growing farming presence as the Irish Bronze Age (c. 2000–c. 400 BC) settles into place.

BRONZE AGE IN GALWAY

Bronze Age newcomers, this time farming folk skilled in the use of metals such as copper and bronze, arrived in County Galway and for nearly two millenniums left their impact on the western landscape.

Initially, these Bronze Age farmers utilised the Wedge Tomb type of burials of the indigenous Neolithic people.

Gradually these newcomers introduced burial in cairns (stone mounds), often on hilltops as at Knockma outside Tuam; tumuli (earthen mounds) such as earthen ring barrows one finds amid the crowded fairways of Athenry Golf Club; and cists (box-like burial compartments) sometimes accompanied by grave goods such as pottery vessels as have been discovered in the past at Annaghkeen near Headford. Many such burial sites have been found in County Galway, with the biggest concentration in the triangle between Tuam, Headford and Athenry, suggesting that this was perhaps the most densely populated area of the county in Bronze Age times.

Funerary monuments as well as land cultivation were not the only intrusions made by these metalworking people on the Galway landscape, however, and while their presence is also noted in the isthmus between Lough Corrib and Lough Mask, where strange formations of standing stones are attributed to them, one sees the greatest concentration of such monuments (over 30) in the aforementioned Cleggan area of Connemara.

These enigmatic standing stones come in circles, in rows (three or more in a line), in pairs or alone, and are now thought to be mainly of a ritual nature. All except the circles are located on hilltops or ridges, are meant to be visible, especially the four-stone row at Derryinver near Tully Cross, and seem to be orientated on major solar and lunar events.

FULACHTA FIADH

Not so visible and only recently discovered are the fulachta fiadh (cooking places of the wild or deer), another set of monuments said to originate in the Bronze Age. They consist of horseshoe-shaped grassy mounds, their cores filled with burnt stone degraded from boiling water in ground troughs inside their perimeters.

These temporary cooking sites are usually located near water sources and, according to general opinion, were used to cook meat in the open. Six were discovered in the laying of the new Galway Eastern Approach Road on the outskirts of the city, and while 17 more are listed in the archaeological inventory of the northern section for County Galway, many more undoubtedly await discovery throughout the entire county area.

CRANNÓGS

Another more prominent monument often associated with Bronze Age settlement is the crannóg, described as a wooden enclosure constructed on a natural or artificial island of stones in lakes or marshy ground. Viewed mostly as defended habitation sites in troubled times, they indicated perhaps the introduction of hostilities at a local level.

Thus, bronze spearheads found on the bed of the River Corrib confirm the changing attitudes of the times, and indicate that the technology for manufacturing weapons of war had settled well in the Galway region. Civilisation had arrived!

In this context, a crannóg was an ideal defensive structure against attack and more are being found every year in County Galway. While 20 or so exist in the Connemara region with perhaps the three Lough Skannive stone examples near Carna being the most prominent, 19 more are in North Galway with the stony remains of the Kiltullagh Lake example near Kilkerrin being a prime example. In the South Galway region a number are clearly evident along the northern shoreline of Loughrea Lake with the high island in the south end of this stretch of water being the most prominent.

CELTS ARRIVE

Into this unsettled context then, in the centuries proximate to the birth of Christ, Ireland saw an infusion of newcomers imbued with a Celtic culture, remnants of which, perhaps, abide more in western behaviour and minds than anywhere else in Ireland today.

The Irish language, still spoken in the Gaeltacht areas of Connemara and the Aran Islands, is a distant link to these restless peoples who felt the power of Rome and came, not as asylum seekers, but in groups eager to implant their way of life on the population in this last Atlantic island.

As well as introducing the worship of natural deities (not forgetting the mysteries of Celtic art as evident on the famous Turoe Stone near Loughrea), these Celtic newcomers also introduced iron technology in the form of weaponry, ploughs and household implements. In doing so they changed for ever the western way of life, and ultimately the landscape.

To them, the point of life was living, and habitation sites took precedence over 'houses of the dead' as they imported into the Galway countryside their strange Celtic philosophy with its laws, rules and customs, and banished the old ways for ever. A warlike people, when cattle were the euro of their day, they gradually introduced the tuatha (tribal) territorial system to the country where new chieftains set up mini kingdoms with hill and cliff forts their initial power bases before the more conventional earthen ringfort came to dominate the landscape.

CELTIC FORTS

Much has been written and a million words debated about the exact function of the famous stone forts on Aran, of which Dún Aengus on Inishmore is the most famous and Dún Conor on Inishmaan one of the most massive, while inland the large hilltop enclosure of Belmont, near Tuam, also furrows the learned brow.

These massive Aran forts in particular, one for each natural division in the three islands, were, it seems, the points of assembly for the inhabitants of each section. Whether it was for defence, seasonal festivals or ceremonies does not trouble the thousands of tourists who come and marvel at these huge stone creations set on the very edge of the world of the time.

RINGFORTS

Smaller circular cashels or cahirs (ringforts of stone) dot this stony Aran landscape also, while on the mainland conventional earthen ringforts or raths are dotted across the arable lands of the county and are thus mostly absent from the mountainy lands of Connemara and the boggy plains of some central and north-eastern areas.

These ancient monuments, dating from c. 400 BC to AD 1600, were simple circular or oval areas surrounded by an earthen bank and scooped-out ditch and usually contained the mud-walled thatched homes of Iron Age or Early Christian farmers and perhaps their extended families. Generally between 20–60 m in diameter, these lightly defended farmsteads acted also as crude stockyards, where animals could be stabled at night safe from predatory man or beast.

In the archaeological inventory of County Galway, the North Galway section alone records 1,104 ringforts with another 840 monuments either levelled or poorly preserved, thus making them the most common antiquity on the Galway landscape today.

Some are of a multivallate nature, having more than just one ditch and bank surrounding them, giving them added status, perhaps reflecting the seat of a local chieftain or even an overlord of a number of tuatha in the district. The massive ringfort at Ballybaan on the eastern outskirts of Galway City may well fall into this latter category, while another large and seemingly well-defended example in the grounds of NUI, Galway on the banks of the River Corrib could have given the title Daingean ('defended area') to the surrounding townland.

DISPERSED CELTIC SETTLEMENT

Either way, they reflect the initial dispersed pattern of Celtic settlement in this Early Iron Age period in County Galway at a time when knowledge of the benefits of a town or even a village was absent from the Irish mindset.

Life was much simpler then with farming the main occupation, and while new ploughing techniques and the advent of the horizontal mill (one at Clybaun on the western outskirts of Galway City has been dated to AD c. 600) increased the importance of cultivation, pastoral care in the form of cattle-rearing remained the main activity of this early rural population.

CELTIC MYTHOLOGY

While archaeology is the most reliable means of revealing antiquity to us, and the early annals, genealogies and poems help unravel the history of County Galway from the seventh century AD onwards, legend and mythology also help us flesh the bones of those who built the monuments of the more distant past. Thus, while we learn that King Guaire, who gave his name to Gort, ruled over South Galway in the seventh century, further west the more mysterious Conmaicne Mara gave Connemara its name.

As one can well imagine, legends also abound amid the long winding inlets and peninsulas of Connemara, with one in particular referring to a fear mór (a giant) after whom the spectacular Great Man's Bay is called. So huge was this giant that tradition even rhymes his fishing exploits:

> His angle-rod made of a sturdy oak,
> His line a cable which in storms ne'er broke;
> His hook he baited with a dragon's tail,
> And he sat upon a rock, and bobb'd for whale.

On a more global scale, mythology in the form of the sagas of Celtic Ireland, still rich in the oral tradition of the ninth century, was copied in works of the twelfth century, especially in the famous Leabhar Gabala (Book of Invasions). Thus, when the Fir Bolgs, the mysterious 'bag men' from Greece, are mentioned as the fourth set of invaders, they left their imprint on the landscape of County Galway. After their defeat at the Battle of Moytura by the men of magic, the Tuatha De Danann, they retreated to Aran and constructed the great stone forts mentioned already, with Aengus, their chieftain, erecting his massive dún on the very edge of the Atlantic cliff face, the famous Dún Aengus of today.

In time, the De Danann, too, were defeated by the Milesians, said to represent the Celts. The fate of the De Danann, this tribe of magical properties, was banishment to underground chambers of the earthen burial mounds, already ancient, it seems, during these legendary dynastic struggles. Not surprisingly they became the sí or síóga (fairies, leprechauns, elves or little people) and came to occupy the mindset of the Irish for generations to come.

Ringforts, defunct since the middle of the second millennium AD, became the 'fairy fort' of modern times, their souterrains or underground passageways the favourite hiding places of these scheming elves living in the parallel world. This 'otherworld' became a favourite topic of conversation around the hearth, especially at night when 'things were about'. The world of the little people was born.

The FIANNA

Meanwhile, another world existed around the campfires of the Fianna, the highly mobile band of warriors in the time of Fionn Mac Cumhaill. One can imagine the heroic tales being canted a thousand times by the bards of old, as simple skirmishes became great battles and heroes even gods on high! Fionn, their famous leader, became a major topic of camp-side tales, as did his thwarted love affair, while the story of his nationwide pursuit of Diarmuid and Gráinne is ingrained in every Irish heart.

The chase came to County Galway, of course, where the great capstones of portal and wedge tombs are still referred locally as Leaba Diarmuid agus Gráinne, the bed of the fleeing couple.

The aforementioned Menlo portal tomb was discovered directly through this title, while on Inishmaan the collapsed wedge tomb beside the airport there also carries the lovers' names, suggesting that water was no barrier to the anger and lust of the legendary Fionn.

Here, as in many other areas in County Galway, archaeology and mythology combine in interpreting the ancient landscape—stones were never lost for words here, and, consequently, Galway is a richer place.

TUATHA DE DANANN

Mythology informs us that the famous navigator of the Tuatha De Danann was Mannanan Mac Lir (the Son of the Sea). In the Galway context he was also known as Orbsen Mac Alloid, after whom Lough Corrib gained its title.

Despite their magical properties, the Tuatha De Danann, who according to legend were eventually defeated by the Celts, fought among themselves, and when Uillin, a grandson of their king, Nuada of the Silver Hand, killed Orbsen in battle on the western shore of Lough Corrib, the place was subsequently called Maigh Uillin (the Plain of Uillin), known today as Moycullen.

The greatest contribution mythology has given to the county, however, is its actual name of County Galway. This, it is suggested by those who dwell in the world of the imagination, originates in the name Galvia. She was a Fir Bolg princess said to have drowned in local waters, since called the Galvia or Galway River—now known as the River Corrib.

ORIGIN OF TITLE 'GALWAY'

Tradition concludes that the Norman town later built upon its eastern banks was called Galvia or Galway in her memory. This is so much nicer than the more historical notation of the word 'Galway' originating in the Gaelic name, Baile na Gaill (the Town of the Strangers), a plausible but rather more mundane version!

Thus, archaeology, mythology and legend play their part in explaining antiquity in the Galway context, before Christian monks stared at seasoned vellum and began to record the spoken word as the second millennium introduced a future still very much based in the past.

Before them, their Celtic equivalents, the Druids, skilled in the magic of the time, exercised complete control over the mind and soul of a people in harmony with the natural gods. Irish antiquity, if one is free to call it that, changed, however, when smoke rose gently on the breeze over a distant hill in Slane in County Meath.

3 CHRISTIANITY

DRUID THEATRE

BEING NOMINATED IN NEW YORK for six Tony awards and winning four with the play *The Beauty Queen of Leenane* was a magical, if rather appropriate, moment in 1998 for the Druid Theatre Company, Galway. Magic, of course, was a favourite ingredient in the daily activities of the ancient Druids, the 'high priests' of Celtic belief, who gave title to Galway's most famous theatrical group. How appropriate then that Druid director, Garry Hynes, who was the first lady to win a Tony for directing, carries a name synonymous with the Uí Fhiachrach Aidhne, the ancient clan of South Galway, whose roots tingle at the mention of anything Celtic.

CELTIC BELIEF

Celtic belief centred on the magical properties of nature. The forces of fire, earth and water were all powerful and governed by gods and goddesses, who were usually benign as long as one catered to their divine needs on a regular basis. The special people ensuring such favoured treatment for and from the gods were, of course, the Druids, learned men who had a special place in Celtic society—favourites of kings and gods alike—of the latter, the Dagda being the most powerful.

Consequently, shining marble temples of the various deities so much favoured by the Romans were absent from the Irish landscape. The gods, through the powers of nature, provided special places of worship amid secret bowers in oakwoods, river sources and pools, and even sacred wells, the latter in particular being much favoured by the Irish.

To become a Druid, one had to be of a special disposition, not least being able to learn the mysteries of that high office, often undergoing an apprenticeship of up to 20 years learning the ancient ways of casting horoscopes, prophesising changes and foretelling the future as well as organising homage to the gods through annual festivals, which were so vital in the lives of the Celts.

CELTIC FESTIVALS

Four major festivals marked the passage from one season to another, and like clergy today the Druids performed special ceremonies relevant to the occasion. The first festival, Samain, celebrated on 1 November, the end of the old year, saw death stain the air. Most of the farm animals were killed just then for winter meat, some the night before as a sacrifice to the gods, thus honouring the 'other' life and heralding Hallowe'en as we know it today. Later Christianised, this festival has Celtic con-notations in the form of games, which still appeal to young people.

The festival of Imbolc, 1 February, the start of spring, was once much celebrated with Galway children going from house to house parading dolls dressed in white to honour the feast of St Bridget or Brigid, said to be the Christian personification of an even earlier Celtic goddess. 'Here's Miss Bridget, dressed in white . . .' went the old refrain, now just a fading memory for the pensioned population.

Next came the festival of Bealtaine on 1 May when Druids drove cattle between twin fires to ward off bovine disease, while homes were decked in bowers of greenery and yellow flowers to welcome the benign influence of the god of sun and growth during the coming summer months. Traces of these customs still exist in the inner streets of Galway City where branches of the May Bush are exhibited over doorways on this day. Ask the owners why this custom persists and the answer 'Sure we always did it' never changes. Ask why it's done, and the silence of the centuries descends!

Finally, 1 August is reserved for the festival of Lughnasa, named after the god Lugh who demanded sacrifices for a rich harvest. Thus, the local population would gather yet again, often on hilltops or mountain passes as at Maumeen near Recess in Connemara, or an even more spectacular example, the greatest Christian alpine outing in Ireland, the annual climb of the 'Reek' or Croagh Patrick in County Mayo. Originally a pagan practice, it now draws countless Galway people on the last Sunday in July each year to join the thousands who gather at the little oratory, built on top of that sacred mountain in 1903, ironically recalling ancient gatherings to honour more ancient gods.

COMING Of ST PATRICK

Today, those who climb the mountain, some 2,500 ft high, do so to honour Ireland's patron saint, St Patrick, who from AD 432 is generally credited with spreading Christianity across this island nation. Doing penance, a sacrifice of self in this onerous climb, is another incentive for the participants to reach the summit where, according to early writings, St Patrick fasted for 40 days and nights.

An affinity with heights was very much the experience of the saint, having spent seven years as a sheep herder on Sliabh Mis in his youthful years as a slave. Yet, it is when he returned to Ireland and lit that paschal fire on the Hill of Slane in opposition to the royal flame on the Hill of Tara that St Patrick first drew official attention to his crusade of converting the Irish to Christianity. His task really started there, and soon he was travelling across the wild countryside of heath, bog and woodland, using rough trackways on top of eskers and toghers over wet lands to visit the various kingdoms on his winding itineraries. Tradition as well as early records will tell you his footsteps sanctified quite a number of places in County Galway.

While on a journey between Cratloe in County Clare and the 'royal palace' in County Roscommon, St Patrick passed along the sides of the Aughty Mountains, stopping briefly in the district of Derrybrien in South Galway. Early ecclesiastical records as well as tradition point to yet another journey through Kiltivna, Dunmore, Kilbannon (where he founded a church), Killower and finally on to Donaghpatrick in North Galway. Here overlooking Lough Hackett and beneath the gaze of the ancient hill of Knockma, with all its magical properties, he founded his main church in the district of Moy Seola, thus naming this important Patrician site Donaghpatrick.

Many other areas in this part of the county claim Patrician connections. Glenamaddy will point the visitor to a little hill in the nearby townland of Gloon called Cnoc na nGlún (Hill of Knees), where the saint is said to have left impressions in the ground while deep in prayer. Not content with that, tradition mentions how he founded the first church in Boyounagh, and having blessed the local well, he used its new sacred waters to baptise local converts.

In East Galway, Ballinasloe has St Patrick and his immediate followers journeying there for the consecration of local son, St Grellan, a favourite student who was, according to records, 'personally instructed, ordained and raised to the episcopate' by the patron himself.

Westwards, however, we have a problem. The Patrician connection here centres mostly on the holy well dedicated to St Patrick on Maumeen Pass when the saint, according to legend, having passed through the Joyce Country to the north, arrived exhausted at this elevated mountain gap. Few souls were to be saved in this vast wilderness, however, and before he departed, he blessed Connemara from on high, but deemed it unnecessary to enter its seemingly empty heart.

ST PATRICK'S LEGACY

Thus, while St Patrick departs these pages to fulfil a divine destiny to the north, his legacy was already taking root, perhaps the firmest in the vast area that is County Galway today. Here archaeology and a rich corpus of oral tradition, later recorded by diligent monks, intermingle to show that while the new faith was gradually reaching souls, ancient pagan traditions were not entirely banished. The hint of compromise was evident as Christianity spread among a people long imbued with a belief in the powerful forces of nature as well as an afterlife of eternal youth.

HOLY WELLS

Water, for example, the source of life itself in the pagan Celtic mind, was not to be sacrificed on the altar of Christian expediency. Sanctuaries such as wells were incorporated into the new religious inventory of places of worship. People continued to gather at these special shrines to thank the new deity for supplying the very essence of life and to commemorate the saint associated with that particular site. The example had been set by St Patrick himself in the high, bubbling waters on Maumeen and in the clear, crystal spring at Boyounagh.

In time, later saints would lend their names to many of the holy wells listed in the archaeological survey of the county, while others with their long tradition of 'patterns' and pilgrimages have simply vanished after falling out of favour with newer generations, such as St Colmcille's Well near Clostoken Church in East Galway, where the last 'rounds' were reported to have taken place in the 1920s. Nevertheless, more than 3,000 holy wells exist in Ireland with over 210 listed in County Galway, manifesting a deep attraction by the rural community in particular for such sites.

Practically every parish boasts at least one holy well, with Lady's Well at Athenry being the most famous in the Galway area. Here on 15 August each year, many people from all over the county as well as from Mayo and Clare gather to participate in the usual 'pattern' around a holy well much embellished in recent times, and now a major centre for Marian devotion in the county.

Another holy well, finely delineated from the surrounding countryside by an elaborate stone bridge structure, is that devoted to a female saint, St Surney, at Drumacoo near Kinvara, as is another dedicated to St Bridget in Loughrea. Perhaps the strangest well adjacent to a holy site is that of Brian Ború, High King of Ireland, situated on a hill beside the early monastic site on High Island off the windswept coast of Claddaghduff in Connemara.

Meanwhile in Castlegar parish, Tobarmacduagh (St Mac Duagh's Well) lies in the townland of Polkeen, while in nearby Cloonacauneen, Tobarrendoney (the Well of the Kings of Sundays) added to the initial attractions of this parish which is now being consumed by the urban spread of Galway City. Holy wells created a problem, however, with much alcohol abuse occurring in their vicinity after the devotions had ended, leading, on strict Church orders, to their eventual abandonment.

Even in Galway City holy wells were rather abundant, with one dedicated to St Brendan usually attended on his feastday, 16 May, by 'the key-street dwellers of old'. The most famous, St Augustine's Well on the shores of Lough Atalia, has recently been restored by the Galway Civic Trust, while two others nearby dedicated to the Blessed Virgin and St John the Baptist have vanished under city developments.

These urban wells were much resorted to in the past, in particular that of St Augustine, when many people gathered on 28 August, his feastday, and carried out certain devotions around it. Several cures were reported for such ailments as ear aches and even blindness. The extraordinary cure of Patrick Lynch, a seriously ill boy, was officially recorded on 23 June 1673. Other holy wells in the town included St Bride's, said to be in the east suburbs, St Bridget's near the present Custom House, St Anne's near Whitestrand Road, while the 'patron' associated with St James's Well at Rahoon had already ceased by the middle of the nineteenth century.

Holy wells, then, or in the Gaelic, 'Uaran', as exemplified in the name, Oranmore, which also has a site with a legendary whiff of a Patrician presence, show the unique affection the Galway Celts had with their pre-Christian past. These revered sites, such as a host of wells dedicated to St Colman in the Kilmacduagh and Gort area of South Galway, St Cuan's Well at Ahascragh, St Grellan's near Ballinasloe, Tobar Ciaráin in Kilkerrin and St Mac Dara's Well on the island of his name off the west coast at Carna, show an unwillingness to break completely with the past, and results in Ireland sporting possibly the highest number of ancient holy wells in the Christian world.

MONASTIC SYSTEM

As the process of conversion, although slow and unspectacular, was spreading across the land, initially it made little impact on the Celtic way of life. The Irish continued to live in ringforts and cashels and to speak the same Celtic language. Chieftains were still inaugurated on the usual sacred sites using the familiar rites of their ancestors, while their holistic way of life from work to leisure hardly varied at all.

Thus, while St Patrick and his religious cohorts did eventually inspire many fervent disciples, their stated aim of founding the Church on an episcopal basis, with dioceses established to correspond as far as possible with combined tuatha, foundered on the Celtic way of life, unique in not having Roman civilisation with all its rules and material advances imposed upon it.

Because of the dispersed nature of Celtic society, without towns or even villages to welcome the advent of a Christian presence, communities ruled by a bishop were difficult to establish in a landscape of scattered habitation. In this unique Irish context Church structure had to mirror life as it was, and missionaries of the new faith literally found the original Irish solution to an Irish problem.

While dioceses still existed and bishops 'retained their dignity of orders', Ireland, and County Galway in particular, witnessed the advent of a simple monastic system spatially dispersed according to the commands of local chieftains, the actual monastic plan echoing the topography and layout of secular habitation sites of the time.

When the first holy men and women, often described as saints in later ecclesiastical writings, came to spread the faith, their preference was for a simple monastic type of site surrounded by the familiar earthen bank or wide stone wall, in the centre of which a humble church building of wood and thatch would be erected to seed the start of Christianity in many sites across County Galway.

Intending to move on to newer pastures after consolidation, eventually these first missionaries would slip quietly to their eternal reward amid the tears of heart-broken monks and simple converts, their final place of interment becoming a place of sanctity and pilgrimage for centuries to come. County Galway has more than its share of such sites, especially in Aran na Naomh (the Islands of the saints), the old title for the Aran Islands.

Other areas included the sheep-dotted eastern shores of Lough Corrib, which in the past have been noted for piety and seats of knowledge. Another section of the county, known for its wealth of Early Christian monastic sites, stretches from Roscam in the eastern suburbs of Galway City south along the eastern section of Galway Bay. Many other singular and often lonely monastic sites, as on the stark Atlantic islands off the Connemara coast, find mention here.

ARAN Of The SAINTS

It is on the three Aran islands stretching majestically across the mouth of Galway Bay that one finds the earliest and greatest concentration of Early Christian monastic sites in County Galway. Here, about the year 483, St Enda, famous for his sanctity and knowledge of the psalms, gathered about him a most important set of scholars whose subsequent influence on the evolving Early Christian Church would be profound. Among them would be some of the first order of Irish saints who, according to tradition, experienced 'cuineas gan uaigneas' (calmness without loneliness), thus avoiding the extreme asceticism practised on other more isolated sites as on High Island off the Connemara coast.

Typical of these saints was the young but hot-tempered Colmcille, who came especially to learn humility under the rule of Enda before embarking on his famous Iona adventure. Finnian of Clonard as well as his namesake of Moville also studied on Aran, as did the great Kieran before he ventured forth to found Clonmacnoise, today the most renowned of all the Early Christian monastic sites. Of local importance we find Jarlath of Tuam and Colman Mac Duagh, later to sow the seeds of Christianity deep in Galway soil. Even the great navigator Brendan is said to have sought advice in this open university to the Creator on Inishmore, as the sacred flame of learning spread initially to the sister isles of Inishmaan and Inisheer.

INISHMORE

Although Enda died about 549 and slumbers now beside 120 other saintly figures of the past in the ruins of his ancient monastic site at Killeany on Inishmore, the largest of the three islands, his legacy lies today in the rich corpus of ruined oratories and small stone churches reminding us of the golden age of Aran na Naomh, which came to a close over a millennium ago.

Many come and say a silent prayer at the sand-covered Teaghlach Éinne at the edge of An Trá Mór on the south-eastern end of Inishmore, a small stone church of the first millennium dedicated to the saint whose foundation lasted for over 500 years until the advent of Viking raiders to the islands at the start of the eleventh century. Typical of its time in size and with its customary antae, which once supported its roof, this humble little church, together with the base of a Round Tower nearby as well as the tiny oratory of Teampall Bheanáin high on the nearby island spine, are all that remain of Enda's monastic settlement, which played such an important part in the founding of the Irish Christian Church.

Fewer, however, undertake the winding climb up to Teampall Bheanáin, regarded by some to be the smallest church in Irish Christendom. Dedicated to St Benin, a disciple of St Patrick, this tiny church high in its exposed position has hardly five metres by two metres of internal space, suggesting rather strongly that penance was very much the goal when its massive masonry was put in place. Congregations would find no room here, of course, with winter winds and rain their constant companions as they huddled in their fervour to assist at Mass celebrated inside, beneath the high-pitched roof so out of proportion to the rest of the tiny building.

In the north of the island, further stony jewels of a pious past dot the rugged landscape such as the quaintly named Na Seacht dTeampaill (the Seven Churches). A scattered cluster of stony artefacts from fragments of High Crosses, incised and plain stone slabs gather around two ancient churches and a number of domestic buildings—the latter indicating that some temporal food did accompany the spiritual way of life in the stern regimen of these Christian pioneers. The main building here, Teampall Bhreacáin (Brecan's Church), is obviously a multi-period structure incorporating a splendid transitional chancel arch leading rather unusually to a chancel of equal breadth with the nave.

As one starts the climb to Dún Aengus at Kilmurvey, note the impressive Teampall Colman Mac Duagh built of massive masonry (one large stone has a horse incised on its surface) in the well-grassed field at the base of the incline. Returning to Kilronan, the main settlement today on Inishmore, four more holy sites deserve attention.

Not far away Teampall Chiaráin stands as a proud memorial to St Kieran, who during his seven years of study on the island absorbed Enda's spirit of endeavour as well as knowledge before founding his own settlement at Clonmacnoise. All around this Aran ruin lie the remnants of early monastic monuments—other buildings, a surrounding wall, cross-inscribed stones and even a stone delineated well—items to be re-created later on a more massive scale on the banks of the

Shannon. As a contrast, a little to the west lies yet another small church, Teampall Asurnaí, dedicated to a female saint whose holy well on the mainland at Drumacoo has already been mentioned.

A final site of importance delights under the title of Teampall an Ceathrar Álainn (the Church of the Four Beautiful Saints), where tradition points to the gable of this ruined building under which the saints, Berchan, Brendan of Birr, Conall and Fursey are said to sleep in Christ beneath four plain slabs. Nearby pillar stones and the obligatory well conclude a rather cursory inventory of Early Christian memorials on Inishmore in its golden age of saints and scholars, which spanned 500 years of piety and learning. The sister islands, too, fell beneath the spell.

INISHMAAN

The main monastic site on Inishmaan (the Middle Island) practically meets the ferry at the island's pier. Cill Cheannannach, the simple church dedicated to St Kenanagh/Gregory is an early oratory of only about 5 m by 3 m in dimension. Built like most of its companions about the end of the first millennium, it contains the customary narrow lintelled doorway with inclined jambs and stone corbels to support the former high-pitched roof. Not far from its bulging north wall, a holed stone rests in the adjacent graveyard, signifying rituals of an even older faith.

INISHEER

Inisheer (the East Island) boasts two sites still to be visited for their historical importance. Teampall Chaomháin, dedicated to the brother of St Kevin of Glendalough, now lies above the island's airstrip, and is unusual in its architectural design. Yet another multi-period structure, the old church is now the chancel area of the new, and the nave the later perhaps thirteenth-century addition, as both snuggle into the sand dunes of time itself.

On the far side of the modern village lies the simple Cill of Gobnet who, according to tradition, came from County Cork. Some early grave slabs and a ruined clochán or circular stone cell lie adjacent to this delightful little oratory, showing perhaps that this female saint carved her own special niche in the male-dominated hierarchy of Aran's holy elite.

OTHER SEA ISLANDS

While these then are just some of the amazing assemblage of Early Christian monuments remaining from the initial surge of Christianity on Aran, other islands off the Galway coast harboured even more remote settlements of monks who saw complete isolation as the perfect way of communing directly with God. Such is St Macdara's little island (c. 60 acres) off the Carna coast in Connemara whose small stone-roofed oratory has recently been fully restored in all its early glamour. The tiny building, famous from its image on recent Irish postage stamps, represents the very best in skeumorphic transformation as it recalls in stone a continuous antae and a carved gable-finial of the wooden proto-type. A major festival in honour of the saint takes place on 16 July, when each passing boat dips its sails three times in honour of this sixth-century man of faith.

Few boats, however, even reach High Island on the wild Atlantic seas where the famous St Feichín of Fore who died in 664 built his early monastery high above the angry seas. Two clocháns (beehive huts) as well as a number of cross-inscribed slabs accompany the little church, all indicating a tiny settlement of monks serving God through the purest form of asceticism. Here, strong Atlantic winds and ocean sprays purged even the purest soul.

LAKE ISLANDS

While other seaward islands off the Galway coast also echoed to the chant of the early monks, inland islands on the great expanse of the Corrib waters too found favour with these initial followers of Christ. Inchagoill, classed as 'the Island of the Devout Stranger' in nineteenth-century tracts, refers, according to tradition, to the founding of the monastic site on this linear wooded island off Oughterard by a nephew of St Patrick. Today, the wood-surrounded settlement contains Teampall Phádraig, a small rectangular stone church with added chancel, while nearby the Saint's Church with its beautiful Romanesque doorway is of later construction.

Most attention, however, centres on the famous 'Luguaedon' Pillar-Stone which contains the inscription, LIE LUGUAEDON MACCI MENUEH. These are some of the earliest carvings of Old Latin characters on stone in the Irish context and have led to much debate among scholars as to the exact wording of the inscription, with some suggesting a pre-Christian meaning.

Further to the east across the great expanse of Corrib water lies Inchiquin, a large flat island now joined to the mainland by a causeway at Greenfields. Here, St Brendan is said to have founded a religious settlement, but the island's main claim to fame is that St Fursey, who filled the dreams of Dante himself and who is Galway's best-known missionary saint, was born here in 584, and to whom an ancient church and graveyard at Killursa is dedicated on the winding road to Headford.

OTHER REGIONS 'FERTILE WITH PIETY'

Southwards along the eastern shores of Lough Corrib during Early Christian times, according to Sir William Wilde, the 'whole of the region was fertile with piety, learning and art'. Chief among the saints mentioned is Cuana whose foundation at Killcoona still boasts the base of a Round Tower, the trademark of an early and important monastic site.

Most attention, however, will focus on 'lovely' Annaghdown, where St Brendan the Navigator came to build a convent for his sister by this delightful verdant inlet of Lough Corrib, and which, sadly, became a place of repose for him when he died there in 577. As the sad cortège left for his final resting place in Clonfert in South Galway, little did the mourners realise how large and important the Annaghdown foundation would become in the subsequent renaissance of the Irish Church.

Meanwhile further north, beyond the fairy hill of Knockma, an early monastic presence was provided by St Benin, a disciple of St Patrick, who founded a monastery at Kilbannon through which the patron saint had passed some years previously. Here again the surviving Round

Tower indicates a site of great antiquity amid these rolling pasture lands of North Galway.

TUAM — RELIGIOUS CENTRE Of COUNTY GALWAY

St Benin was not alone in his endeavours. In the fifth century a young St Jarlath from the district of Dunmore took his first steps to sainthood. After ordination he established his own monastery at Cloonfush, where St Brendan came to interpret his rather troubled dreams. Thus, when Jarlath's chariot broke a wheel at Tuaim Dhá Ghualainn (the Mound of the Two Shoulders), he knew from Brendan's words that here he should found his major settlement devoted to God.

The divine word came to Jarlath at Tuam, where it would thrive as nowhere else in Galway. Not surprisingly Jarlath's foundation would become the seat of archbishops and even kings in the changing times that followed. Today the remains of a High Cross and the magnificent Hiberno-Romanesque arch in St Mary's Cathedral remind us of these hallowed days when the triangular area of Tuam, Kilbannon and Donaghpatrick evolved under such strong Patrician beginnings.

OTHER EARLY ECCLESIASTICAL CENTRES

Most other areas in County Galway have saintly associations, such as Clonfert founded by St Brendan about 560 which, because of its importance, later became a bishopric. This is seen also in names such as Tynagh and Tiaquin, from the Irish 'teach' (house), Isertkelly from 'díseart' (a hermitage), while Cill or Kil as in Kilconnell and Kilchreest is the most common term indicating a church or monastic site in early Irish placenames.

Although no Early Christian presence has been detected in the inner Galway City area, an important corridor of faith ran south along the eastern shores of Galway Bay. A monastic site at Roscam under St Odran on the eastern outskirts is simply brimming with monuments associated with the period. Although the ruined church there is much later, the presence of a huge encircling wall, Round Tower and two large bullaun stones for grinding materials indicate the importance of the Early Christian site. They also point to the start of yet another region noted for its piety and learning.

Just south of Oranmore is Caherdrineen, a stone enclosure nestling beside the main Galway/Gort road, with an interesting Early Christian carving of an anchor on one of the large boulders incorporated in the wall, while nearby lies part of the shaft of an eight/ninth-century High Cross. Further on Kilcolgan, whose name suggests yet another early monastic site, one founded by St Colgan, has a whole plethora of place-names in its vicinity such as Killeely with St Foila as its patroness, Killeeneen and Kiltiernan, all referring to a firm rooting of Christianity in its early phases in this locality. Nearby, the Drumacoo monastic site on the Kinvara Road also falls within this area of piety and learning, its aforementioned holy well dedicated to St Surney.

Kiltiernan is perhaps the most interesting of these early monastic sites because its internal area of 1.4 hectares contains a large, partially restored pre-Romanesque church over 16 m in length, complete with trabeate doorway. Even today the outlines of up to 20 structures, mostly house-sites, can still be discerned under grassy mounds, which also reveal up to 16 sub-enclosures mostly radiating out from the near centre church site. Although one of the few excavated monastic sites in the county, doubts remain as to whether this ancient monastery was founded by Tiernan in the fifth century or, according to local tradition, by St Colman Mac Duagh in the seventh century.

KILMACDUAGH

As regards Colman's greatest foundation, however, there can be no doubt. Kilmacduagh, just outside Gort in South Galway, is the county's most famous early monastic site, easily noted against the grey, austere background of the Burren in nearby County Clare. Its point of reference is its famous Round Tower over 100 ft in height, Ireland's Leaning Tower of Pisa, inclined almost a metre from the perpendicular.

Although a large cluster of more recent church buildings blanket this sacred site chosen by Colman where, according to tradition, his belt fell to the ground, only its ruined cathedral extending over an earlier church complete with blocked-up trabeate west doorway, and a rather enigmatic stone building outside the modern cemetery said to be associated with St Colman, as well as the Round Tower itself, refer to the Early Christian period.

It's enough, of course, because the final docking of the new faith with the hearts and minds of Galwegians is reflected rather well in the crumbling stones of Kilmacduagh, The 'hopeless superstition' of the Irish is echoed in the long veneration of its holy well and of the sacred tree planted there by the saint himself. Folklore is very much alive in the story of Colman's belt and the Gobán Saor erecting Galway's sixth Round Tower there. The growth of the monastery after Colman's death is evident in the later spread of medieval buildings, drawing visitors constantly to the music of the psalms, which have never really gone away.

4 MEDIEVAL TIMES

RECORDING T*h*e PAST

FOR T*h*OSE WISHING TO LEARN, the recording of history is like the journey of a train rumbling through the past. Up to the end of the first millennium the pre-history of County Galway has come mainly from the fruits of archaeology and oral tradition. Yet it was only early in the second millennium, when learned scribes began to record annual events as they occurred as in the *Annals of Connacht* (AD 1224–1544), that the train began to run, each station stop a yearly milestone in the story of time.

Archaeologists, encouraged by the efforts of nineteenth-century antiquarians, only began to play their part within the last hundred years or so. The oral tradition on the other hand, with all its myths, sagas and imaginative licences, found favour with the scribes a thousand years ago when holy men saw beyond the illuminated Latin manuscript and began to record the Gaelic mantras of the filidh, the bardic poets of the old tradition, who with the brehons (lawyers) replaced the Druids as keepers of knowledge in the changing order.

Thus while Irish archaeology, through the scientific scrutiny of monuments and artefacts, can tell what happened 'on the ground' before writing commenced, it finds it near impossible to wed the identity of occupiers with sites such as ringforts and crannógs. Even oral tradition would not attempt to do so in every case, but the filidh were not afraid to fill many of the petty kingdoms with tribal names, while the information they supplied is overpowering in its simplicity in explaining what happened in Ireland before history began to be properly recorded.

The filidh, as well as reciting poetry, were the mental keepers of the past, who learned the ancient sagas and tribal genealogies by rote and were delighted to find new and eager listeners in the confines of the scriptorium. Thus while the earliest surviving manuscripts are Latin copies of the Gospels and Psalms, later vellums tell in Gaelic the story of the Irish race back to the Flood.

WRITTEN HISTORY

Annals of the Four Masters and the famous range of Lecan volumes as well as Leabhar Genealach (the Book of Genealogies) written by Duald Mac Firbus in the Church of St Nicholas in Galway City, all recall a time when Connacht was one of five provinces of Ireland, the fifth being North Leinster with Tara its royal centre.

Meanwhile, Cruachain in County Roscommon became the Connacht equivalent as various western kingdoms combined in times of conflict, when the iron sword was the weapon of the moment and cattle the currency of the day.

UÍ FHIACHRACH TERRITORIES

In the first millennium after Christ tribal territories associated with County Galway figure in the narratives with Uí Fhiachrach territories and tribes finding early mention. Fiachra was a fifth-century pagan king of Connacht whose famous son Daithí was killed by lightning at the foot of the Alps. While the Uí Fhiachrach Muaidhe area was possessed mainly by the O'Dowd clan, whose lands extended from Sligo down to the River Robe, the southern Uí Fhiachrach Aidhne or Theas covered mostly South Galway. Eoghan Aidhne, who was a grandson of Daithí, had his eldest son Conall act as progenitor of the four important tribal families of the southern Uí Fhiachrach, the O'Hynes, O'Shaughnessys, O'Clerys and Kilkellys. Of these the O'Hynes became the most dominant with dúns or earthen forts at Ardrahan and Kinvara acting initially as their major centres of power.

Subsequently, and one can almost hear the ancient bards listing off the names, many of the Uí Fhiachrach Aidhne became kings of Connacht, even attaining the high kingship itself with, as one might guess, 'opposition'. Of these Guaire Aidhne, who held court in the seventh century, was famous for his many battles especially on the borders with Clare, but was reviled for his part in the murder of a kinsman, St Ceallagh, the 'Prince Bishop of Kilmore Moy', thus precipitating a breakdown in relations with the northern Uí Fhiachrach.

Yet there was a benign side to Guaire, whose earthen ringfort adjacent to the present Dunguaire Castle at Kinvara was once described as 'the white-sheeted fort of soft stones, habitation of poets and bishops' in early records. By all accounts he was a generous patron of the arts as well as the clergy, with his right hand longer than the other from the 'unremitting exercise of generous beneficence'. It was he who encouraged St Colman Mac Duagh to found a monastery in his kingdom, which the latter did at Kilmacduagh. Guaire also extended his royal presence southwards to a fort, about which the town of Gort, still delighting in its Irish name of Gort Inse Guaire (the Field on Guaire's Island), was later built. Guaire died in 662, and after the death of his grandson Feargeal Aidhne, the Connacht crown passed from the Uí Fhiachrach Aidhne to the Uí Bhrian tribes whose territories lay mostly in North Galway.

Oral tradition, much of it now secured in the recordings of the scribes, refers to other early tribal activities in County Galway, where information on warring kingdoms, cattle-raiding as well as genealogies are found in Irish libraries and in European centres of education, where Irish monks helped conserve the Christian faith during the Dark Ages.

OTHER GALWAY CLANS

Conflict was certainly in the air when St Grellan, a pupil of St Patrick, intervened with warring tribes verging on the River Suck near Ballinasloe and helped settle the Uí Máine in this far eastern corner of

County Galway. Of these the O'Kellys later became the most dominant sept, especially in the middle of the county, their territory stretching east from Athenry to Ballinasloe. The O'Maddens were another branch of the Uí Máine, centred mostly in the south-eastern part of the county, especially around the present town of Portumna; while the O'Fahy and Lally clans occupied the territory around Loughrea, the latter moving northwards towards Tuam after the Norman invasion. While many of the later Tower Houses or castles can be associated with these families, few ringforts can be assigned to them in these early years of clan formation.

This is true also regarding clan consolidation in the Connemara area of the county. Connemara is the modern name for Conmaicne Mara, the descendants of Conmac who chose to live by the western sea. Led by the Ó Cadhla tribe, later the Keeleys, other early clans associated with Connemara included the Conneelys (with all the various spellings of the name), the Mac Conry of Gnomore and the O'Adhnaidh of Gnobeg, both verging on the western shores of Lough Corrib. Later groups such as the O'Hallorans, Lees, O'Tooles and even the penultimate overlords of the province, the O'Flahertys, finally ousted by the Martins, all played their part in the history of Connemara, whose spatial expanses of mountain, lake and vale could easily constitute a county on its own as its borders are clearly delineated by nature.

O'FLAHERTY CLAN

The O'Flahertys, one of the most famous of the clans associated with Galway, initially occupied the rich lands known as Moy Seola east of Lough Corrib before their expulsion westwards into Connemara by the Normans in the thirteenth century.

Not much is known about their actual land possessions in Moy Seola except that the Annals mention them as lords of that territory stretching from near Tuam south towards Athenry and westwards to Lough Corrib. The earliest reports about the clan refer to them as Muintir Murchadha, from Morogh, who died in 891, a descendant of Duach Galach, a son of King Brian and brother of the aforementioned Fiachra. Thus, many Connacht clans are all collateral branches of the same family stretching back to the earliest references of the filidh.

The O'Flahertys subsequently derived their clan name from Flaherty, a fifth-generation leader further down the family tree. It should be noted also that the O'Flahertys acted as overlords to other clans verging on Moy Seola, now the Barony of Clare, such as the O'Hallorans who held, according to the Annals, 'the twenty-four townlands of Clan Fergail', an area immediately east of the River Corrib. This family, too, descended from Eochaidh Muighmeadhon who died in 366, the great father figure of all the leading clans of Connacht.

EARLY GALWAY CITY FORTS

It is not possible to equate actual settlement sites with the O'Flahertys or the O'Hallorans, but the large enclosed site of the multivalleted ringfort at Ballybaan on the outskirts of Galway City may well have been an O'Halloran settlement. Also, the tree-covered ringfort on the university campus by the western bank of the River Corrib has led to some debate over the original occupiers, but perhaps it gives the title Daingean (a defended place) to the townland.

More intriguing was the recently demolished ringfort once situated on a nearby hillock overlooking both the Corrib and Galway Bay at Rahoon, which has been interpreted as the 'Fort of Ún', thus giving title to the important modern city parish. Who Ún was is not known, but the spur of rock, which once formed the fort's base can still be seen adjacent to the new housing development at Grangemore. Sadly, a meeting with a modern mechanical digger has been more devastating than all the vicissitudes encountered by this old fort down through the centuries, including perhaps attack from the Vikings, the first invaders to visit these shores in post-Celtic times.

ARRIVAL Of The VIKINGS

The arrival of the Vikings in Ireland is well documented, and it is now realised that it was the Norse from Norway and not the Danes who should bear our odium for Viking onslaughts on this island. From the first hostile incursions at Lambay Island off Dublin in 795 to the final adoption of the Irish way of life at the close of the eleventh century, the Vikings have contributed much to Irish history, not least in the sacking of monastic sites, founding towns and introducing coinage. In County Galway they came as plunderers—and paid the price.

The earliest Galway reference to these Norse invaders points to the year 816 when they raided the monasteries in North Clare before marching through County Galway, laying havoc in their wake as they moved from Kilmacduagh to Oranmore and on to Lough Corrib. In 835 Turgesius, perhaps the most noted leader, ravaged the entire province of Connacht. In 866 another large force landed near Kilcolgan, and one can imagine the damage done to monastic sites in that district during this incursion.

The tenth century saw no let-up in these attacks on religious as well as secular sites in County Galway, with new evidence showing Viking activity along the Connemara coastline. In 928 the 'foreigners of Luimneach [Limerick] went up the Lough Orbsen [Corrib], and the islands of the lake were plundered by them' we are told in the rather clipped reporting style of the Annals. By then the Vikings had established a settlement at the mouth of the Shannon, thus laying the foundation of Limerick City, and were eager to plunder the rich harvests of gold and grain in ecclesiastical targets ranging from Kilmacduagh to Inchagoill on Lough Corrib.

However, these hostile incursions eventually came at a price and, not surprisingly, we learn that in 938 Harold, Viking king in Limerick, was killed by the chieftain of the Hynes clan at Raheen in the parish of Ardrahan. Meanwhile a Viking burial complete with weapons has been discovered at Eyreport shore near Clifden, where the skeleton of a tall young Scandinavian was interred in the sand along with a shield, a sword, a dagger and a spear. He is now a star exhibit in the National Museum of Ireland!

Folklore up to recent times recalled the Viking presence on Lough Corrib with mysterious 'pointed' boats on the bed of the lake accepted as 'proof positive' of Scandinavian activity on these normally tranquil waters. As well, corroding Viking-type weapons together with human skeletal remains and even sling shot, a favourite weapon of the Irish, have been found on the bed of the River Corrib near the Dangan ringfort, suggesting that the native clans of the time were anything but friendly towards these foreign newcomers at the end of the first millennium.

This may explain why the Vikings never founded a settlement at the mouth of the River Corrib, where an Poll Mór (Large Hole), in more recent times the Dún Aengus Dock, would have made a safe anchorage for their longboats as they contemplated the rich harvests further upstream. Galway City would wait a few more centuries before other more forceful strangers would turn the quiet estuarine settlement into a prosperous medieval port.

Thus by the close of the first millennium, clan politics was much too volatile on the Galway home front for the Vikings and their Irish descendants to play a part, as Tuam evolved into the ecclesiastical centre of the region, while the O'Flahertys and O'Heynes saw another collateral branch of the founding fathers of Connacht, the O'Connors, rise to power not only in the province but even to the high kingship of Ireland itself.

O'CONNOR KINGS

Again we must look to Eochaidh Muighmeadhon who, according to the Annals, 'died king of Ireland, AD 366', as progenitor of the O'Connor clan through his son Brian. As the first millennium drew to a close, the Uí Bhrian we are told had 'vast patrimonial domains in Connacht, and generally had the suffrages of the provincial states [such as the O'Flahertys] in the election of provincial kings of the province'.

As one might expect, the Uí Bhrian subdivided with the main branch, the Clan Murray, descending from Murrach Mullethan, king of Connacht, who died in 702. Much later, in 1030, another leader of this section, Teige, adopted the surname of Ua Conchobhar (O'Connor). Since then it has become the royal family surname of Connacht, delighting in many derivatives, and has seen high kings (with opposition) and in modern times golfers (with scratch handicaps) gain national and international recognition.

With their main seat of power in Roscommon, the O'Connor impact on the Galway landscape is rather weak. Only a portion of a tower or turret known as the 'Chair', thought to be part of the 'Wonderful Castle' erected by them in Tuam and said to be the first stone castle erected in Ireland, indicates their secular presence in Tuam. Nearby in Dunmore, from the Gaelic Dún Mór (Big Fort), the later Norman castle rises high above a raised earthen defensive site, a suggested stronghold of Turlough O'Connor (1088–1156), the first of the O'Connors to become High King of Ireland. This earthen fort at Dunmore and the stone castle in Tuam may mark the western edge of the actual O'Connor kingdom before the advent of the Normans in 1169 changed the structure of land tenure in Ireland for ever.

CHURCH REORGANISATION

On the ecclesiastical front a huge reformation was already taking place during the twelfth century as the old monastic system felt the wind of change blowing across from continental Europe, where Christianity was busy reinvigorating itself after the Dark Ages. The O'Connor chieftains played no small part in participating in this renewal of the faith by lending their support to the administrative as well as the physical changes taking place within the Irish Church, already weakened by conflict and discontent.

Conflict came in two forms, with the physical variety already evident in the repeated plunderings of the monasteries by Viking as well as warring Irish clans. Burnings of the wooden churches of the time helped lead to stone structures making a rather belated appearance on the Irish landscape, while Round Towers, built originally as 'bell-towers' in monastic enclosures, soon displayed defensive features with entrances inserted high above ground level, as is evident in Kilmacduagh. That troubled times were impinging on monastic life is evident from the unfinished state of the Round Tower at Roscam, while Galway's other examples are at Killeany on Aran, Ardrahan, Kilbannon and Kilcoona.

The main conflict came from within, however, with some monastic complexes seeking corporal rather than spiritual advancement, where the rule of the abbot/prince became much removed from the pious teachings of the founding saint. By the start of the twelfth century the old monastic establishment had grown weary of itself. Reform filled the Irish air encouraged by great changes taking place in the Church throughout Europe at the start of the second millennium AD.

Recovering from the trials of the Dark Ages, continental Christianity renewed itself with fresh vigour, and this new spirit of religious reform found expression in Ireland via various synods such as at Rathbreasail in 1111, which introduced a new Church organisation based on dioceses, bishoprics and parishes, replacing the old Irish monastic system. Connacht received five sees with Cong initially, it seems, designated its diocesan centre. The later Synod of Kells in 1152 saw the archdiocese centre on Tuam, long looked on as the true religious heart of the county whose pulse was first set in motion by St Jarlath half a millennium before. Kells sealed its place in the new order, a position it treasures to the present day.

Church reform was evident in other ways as well with the introduction of the new Religious Orders, whose continental fervour in respreading the word of Christ in its truest form manifested itself in a massive building boom in churches, with an exciting Romanesque architecture to match.

NEW CHURCH ARCHITECTURE *and* ORDERS

While the small wooden churches of the earlier Irish period were gradually replaced by stone versions with chancels added, a new and exciting church-building programme was introduced in the twelfth century by the Cistercians, the first of the new Orders to arrive. When St Malachy introduced the new monastic church enclosure to Mellifont in 1142, it simply reinforced official enthusiasm for such religious ventures already set in motion by King Cormac MacCarthy who had the beautiful Cormac's Chapel built on the historic Rock of Cashel in 1134. The Romanesque style of architecture had arrived.

Parish churches and cathedrals vied with the new monastic centres of the main incoming Orders of Cistercians, Benedictines, Dominicans and Franciscans in architecture as well as presence. In this regard the finest examples of Irish Romanesque are evident in three County Galway cathedrals. Clonfert boasts of the most exciting doorway of its type with six orders incorporating a fine display of motifs ranging from animal and human heads to delightful geometric designs, while overhead an overpowering array of carved human heads completes this amazing study in Irish stone ornamentation.

In 'lovely' Annaghdown, its twelfth-century cathedral has, in the minds of many, the most exquisite Hiberno-Romanesque window with its curved carving of an animal following faithfully the round of the window top, unfazed by the delicacy of design all about it. The window has been described as a memorial to genius and the fertility of mental conception.

Chancel arches also provided an inspirational source for the new ornamentation, and at St Mary's Cathedral in Tuam Romanesque design shines forth again. Although fire destroyed the original church, the arch survives in the present nineteenth-century building. Its six orders are crowned by ornamentation hardly surpassed in Ireland, the faces on its capitals a study in carving at its most whimsical.

Yet it was in the arrival of the Religious Orders and the setting up of their new style monasteries alongside the benign influence of the O'Connor kingship extending to these radical innovations in church structure that we see the changes take place in the built landscape. While High King of Ireland, Turlough Mór O'Connor is said to have built Cong Abbey for the Canons Regular of St Augustine after 1137. (His son Ruairi died there in 1198.) Not long after, about 1140, he founded the Augustinian Priory of St John the Evangelist in Tuam. Meanwhile his other son, Cathal Crobhdhearg, established the famous abbey at Knockmoy with its unique line paintings of saints and kings for the Cistercians who came from Boyle in 1189–90.

Other monasteries founded under Irish patronage included Clontuskert Priory of the Canons Regular of St Augustine, which received much favour from the local O'Kelly chieftains, as did the Franciscan Friary at Kilconnell which was founded by William O'Kelly in 1353. Meanwhile, the O'Maddens were involved in the transfer of the Cistercian foundation at Portumna to the Dominicans, which saw Pope Martin V grant a Bull in 1426 confirming the takeover; while at Annaghdown the monastery there was granted to the Arroasian nuns shortly after 1195.

CHURCH ENDOWMENTS BY NORMAN INVADERS

The main promotion of the new Orders came from a new and frightening source, however, as the first waves of a twelfth-century Norman invasion began to impact on County Galway. The year was 1169 when these invaders came ashore in the south-east of Ireland, but

it was not until the start of the thirteenth-century that their repres-
entatives, de Burgo barons, deceitful grantees of the province of
Connacht by the Crown, finally took forceful possession of County
Galway. As if to assuage a collective guilty conscience, both the de
Burgos and their followers found comfort in establishing even more
monasteries for the incoming Orders in the new territories.

At Loughrea, where Richard de Burgo, overlord of the Norman invaders
in the Connacht region, set up a major settlement in his primary manor
in the thirteenth century, we find the Carmelites being invited and
given the means to found a priory there. In time Loughrea would
become one of Galway's important medieval towns with some of the
remains of the original fosse and a wall tower still visible today.

To the west, Sir William de Burgo, surnamed Liath (Grey), founded a
friary for the Franciscans in 1296 on an island on the northern outskirts
of the embryonic medieval town of Galway, an establishment that was
much endowed in the following centuries by its rich merchants, subsequently called the 'Tribes of Galway'. Later, and to the north beyond
the present town of Headford, we find the extensive ruins of Ross Errilly,
a major Franciscan Friary said to have been founded by Sir Raymond
de Burgo in 1351. The new power in the region, the de Burgos were
continuing the example set by their predecessors, the O'Connor High
Kings, who gradually fade from this history as family struggles took their
toll in the face of the new invasion.

The main supporters of the de Burgos, the de Berminghams, were also
to the fore in welcoming and endowing various branch houses of the
new Religious Orders. In their main defended settlement, the town of
Athenry, we find Meiler de Bermingham, classed as the 2nd Lord of
Athenry, founding a friary dedicated to Saints Peter and Paul for the
Dominicans in 1241. We have to wait, however, until 1425 to see Walter
de Bermingham, then described as the Lord Baron of Athenry, founding
a friary for the Augustinians in Dunmore, long a seat of power of the
O'Connors. By then, of course, the old political order was changing fast.

Lesser Norman families such as the de Cogans also invited the
Religious Orders into their newly acquired territories. Thus in 1250, they
were gracious in their invitation to the Franciscans to found yet another
friary, this time in Claregalway, a house which was subsequently much
endowed by the munificence of the nearby de Berminghams in
Athenry. A market also grew up about this friary, whose ruins are such a
dominant feature of this satellite village of Galway City today.

EARLY NORMAN INCURSIONS

Dominance, of course, was the key to survival in these dangerous times of the late twelfth century as the O'Connor kings faced a conflict unvisited on the region since the demise of the Vikings some centuries earlier. Foreigners were at the entrances of Irish forts again. This time taking no for an answer was not an option as Irish might faded before Norman armour, and later to the English longbow.

Practically every school-goer has learned how Diarmait Mac Murchada first invited Norman help at a time when English barons were casting covetous eyes across the Irish seas. Land was there for the taking, and this timely invitation saw the first of these adventurers land in the south-east in 1169, followed shortly after by a more formidable invasion force led by Richard de Clare, better known as Strongbow, and in 1171 by King Henry II himself. With the help of an army of 4,000 men, Henry swept through Leinster, taking even Dublin before Roderic O'Connor, monarch of Ireland and king of Connacht, finally acted against him. However, due to incessant internal quarrelling, Roderic was defeated and sued for peace.

Thus the pattern for centuries to come was initiated: internal dissension among the Irish—defeat—honourable terms granted and subsequently dishonoured. While Roderic was permitted to continue as king of Connacht, the province was later granted surreptitiously to the powerful de Burgo family in 1215. Prior to that, other Normans tried their hand at invading the region on the invitation of various sections of the warring O'Connor clan, which saw the kingship of Connacht alternate in anger between Roderic and his brother, Cathal Crobhdhearg, as well as their various offspring. Such internecine conflicts among the ruling Irish provided short-term but bountiful gains for the Normans— they also signalled disaster if the timing was wrong.

When Milo de Cogan entered Connacht at the invitation of one of Roderic O'Connor's sons, he was defeated by the rest of the O'Connor clan in 1178, as was Hugo de Lacy in 1181. About the year 1200 William ('The Conqueror') de Burgo invaded Connacht on an invitation from Cathar O'Connor to help him fight his kin, Cathal Crobhdhearg. According to the Annals they left 'neither church nor territory that they did not pillage or destroy'.

The following year we find William fighting on the side of Cathal Crobhdhearg, but by 1204 the sides were at war with each other yet again. As ever, civilians and humble monks paid a terrible price, with the Annals of Clonmacnoise noting: 'AD 1204. William Burke took the spoils of the churches of Connacht.' Specifically named were the County Galway churches of 'Clonfert, Milick, Kilbenan, and Tuam', with Knockmoy being attacked the previous year. Although it was a foretaste of what was to come, permanent settlement by the Normans was not yet fully possible due to the volatility of the O'Connors.

All such incursions were mostly unsuccessful as in 1225 when a rather famous victory was celebrated by the 'Irish' at Ardrahan. Here we learn that the Normans had occupied the old seat of the O'Heynes, allies of the O'Connors. The latter immediately sought a Connacht hosting against the aggressor, gathering warriors from their own clan, the neighbouring O'Flahertys of Moy Seola and, rather appropriately, the O'Dowds from Sligo. For the last time the descendants of the Uí Fhiachrach Muaidhe, the O'Dowds, came south to support those of the Uí Fhiachrach Aidhne with, according to various translations from the Annals, Taichleach O'Dowda personally dispatching the 'constable of the English'! The rest, of course, is musical history, with this particular victory celebrated from Boston to Birmingham in the popular song, 'The West's Awake'.

RICHARD DE BURGO

But sadly the West was never quite awake to the dangers presented by the de Burgos, whose adventurous intent to possess Connacht (they were already granted Munster) intensified in that same year of 1225 when young Richard de Burgo, who succeeded his father William in 1205, received the royal nod yet again, thus degrading even further the original grant of the province made years before to Roderic O'Connor. That royal intrigue was always in the air can be seen when Cathal Crobhdhearg was granted Connacht, while on the same day, 13 September 1215, Richard de Burgo was given a similar grant!

It all came to a head when Feidhlim, the son of Cathal Crobhdhearg, came to the Connacht throne in 1230 with de Burgo help, and while initially siding with the 'gall' (foreigners), he was eventually imprisoned at their new castle at Meelick for breaking guarantees of loyalty. Released by royal decree, Feidhlim soon reverted to his old ways, attacking in

1233 for instance the reinforced de Burgo fortification at the mouth of the River Corrib, previously seized from Hugh O'Flaherty.

Enough was enough, and in 1235, instead of trying to placate the warring O'Connors once again, Richard de Burgo assembled a powerful army of Norman might including forces of the justiciar, Maurice Fitzgerald, as well as those of Hugh de Lacy, the Earl of Ulster, and began with a decisive campaign the final conquest of a troublesome Connacht. While the fortified settlement at the mouth of the River Corrib subsequently felt the ire of more O'Connor attacks, the overall trend in the following decades was a blanket colonisation of the finest lands in Connacht by the Normans, with the O'Connors confined to the King's Five Cantards eventually granted to them in the east of the province, now County Roscommon. A visit by Feidhlim O'Connor to Henry III in 1240 combined with the efforts of his son Áed at reconciliation, leading to lessening confrontations with the occupying forces, were manifestations of a much-reduced O'Connor power. The old Gaelic order was changing, with the new colonists leaving their military mark on western landscapes, as the O'Connors slip quietly from these pages for the moment.

CONQUEST and CONSOLIDATION

Colonisation comes in binary form however—conquest and consolidation. While the Normans were quite successful in the former, they never quite achieved the latter where County Galway was concerned. In the initial phase of conquest their primary incursions, as mentioned in the Annals, met with only temporary success. Proof of this is the sparse number of their war monuments identified in the county today.

In all only six mottes or steep-sided earthen mounds, once complete with wooden towers or castles on top and surrounded by wooden palisades, have been identified in County Galway. Thrown up quickly, they were utilised as small fortified garrisons on the conquest trail, designed to cope with any counter-attacks from local clans. The fact that only six exist in the county, mostly in the south-east, suggests they may have been part of earlier sorties prior to 1235 when the main Norman invasion of Connacht began.

From that year onwards permanent occupation was clearly indicated by the erection of two-storey stone 'hall-houses' (the first real 'castles' in native dialect), with thick walls and entry only at first-floor level by an external staircase and a fortified doorway. Thus no battering ram could be used to gain entry, and access to the ground floor where provisions were kept was completely internal from the main living hall on top.

These stone castles represent the earliest military intent to establish permanent settlements by the Normans under de Burgo overlords, and were deliberately placed at strategic points of access and defence throughout County Galway to achieve maximum dominance of the surrounding countryside as quickly as possible. Thus, when the O'Flahertys were forced westwards across Lough Corrib, perhaps the earliest form of ethnic cleansing in the Galway context, stout Norman hall-houses were placed at Annaghkeen and Cargin (the latter recently renovated into a fine guest house!) on the eastern shores of the lake to ensure the permanent expulsion of the dominant Irish clan from Moy Seola.

EARLY GALWAY CITY STRUCTURES

A major fortification at the mouth of the River Corrib also achieved this purpose as well as laying the foundation of the settlement, which would become the medieval town of Galway. Meanwhile its nearby aisled-hall discovered in recent excavations under the Custom House at Flood Street has its doorway at ground level, indicating a safe environment behind the rise of the great town wall. This was part of the settlement, which would evolve into the medieval town of Galway after 1270. This hall may even have become the defence centre of the de Burgos as Irish insurgence measures began to dismantle the fruits of the initial conquest.

O'CONNOR THREAT FROM The NORTH

The main threat, always inherent from the blighted ambitions of the O'Connors, lay in the northern areas of the county. Here, Richard de Burgo, son of William 'The Conqueror', placed his chief tenants, the de Berminghams, whose hall-houses at Athenry (their main centre) and at Dunmore were later enhanced by the extra storeys we see today.

On this northern line of defence also is Moylough hall-house, now a ruin of three storeys within the remains of a rectangular enclosure. When erected in the thirteenth century, it was in the control of the de Coterels, themselves tenants to the de Berminghams, as the feudal sytem spread its close-knit defensive network across the lands of high agricultural value in East Galway.

SOUTHERN THREAT

Meanwhile to the south, although the O'Heynes had a declining presence around Ardrahan, in nearby County Clare lay the wild O'Briens, always a military threat. At Ardrahan, already a settlement (and Kilcolgan with potential as a port), we find Maurice Fitzgerald being granted Uí Fhiachrach Aidhne in 1235, and today the crumbling remains of his castle at Ardrahan beside the main Galway/Limerick road is a stark reminder of these unsettled times. Even here the de Burgo presence was never far away, as is evident in the rather dour remains of another of their early castles at Ballinacourty, and the more impressive ruin of an even larger family castle at nearby Kiltartan.

NORMAN DEFENCE STRUCTURES

In all, some 26 of these early Norman castles have been identified in County Galway, with the main building phase starting about 1230. Although some castle destruction has been recorded in the Annals from this time onwards, the march to colonisation was irreversible, with the manorial system in operation and various classes of tenants accommodated.

The manorial lord, a main tenant of the de Burgos, lived in one of the aforementioned castles or in the larger of 55 moated sites which dot the best farming lands of East Galway. Moated sites were square or rectilinear defended habitation sites, defined by a wide water-filled ditch. In Galway the smaller ones were isolated farmhouse settlements of the larger free-tenants, usually set away from the evolving Norman urban settlements known as villages, boroughs and towns.

Various strategic sites were granted weekly markets and an annual fair by its feudal lord and gradually grew into villages. Those showing promise of further expansion such as Ardrahan, Claregalway, Kilcolgan, Kilcorban, Meelick, Portumna, and even Tuam, an Early Christian and a unique Irish settlement, were given borough status with promised privileges such as a corporation and free citizenship acting as incentives to attain full medieval town status. A town would be further defined by having as extras, a castle, defensive walls, a church, street and burgess plot patterns, and a whole ancillary set of facilities such as bridges, quays, seats of religious orders, etc. as appropriate to its topography.

FOUNDING OF FOUR MAIN TOWNS

In the early excitement of the Norman conquest of County Galway, however, only four towns evolved under their stewardship, with Loughrea initially the most important, being the chief seat of the de Burgo lordship, while Athenry and, to a lesser extent, Dunmore enjoyed de Bermingham patronage. On the western periphery of the colonised areas, the castle of Bun Gaillimhe on the Galway (now Corrib) River mouth, developed by Richard de Burgo in the early 1230s on an earthen fort erected there in 1124 by Turlough O'Connor, was the chief incentive for a former fishing settlement to grow quickly into a town.

Protection for family and possessions was an important factor in seeing this, the most western of the 12 urban centres envisaged by the Normans for the county, grow into the powerful medieval city-state of Galway. Already defended on three sides by water, this peninsular settlement site needed only a massive wall-building programme to begin in 1270, a local market augmented by a natural port facility, and an influx of merchant burghers, for the de Burgos to make this their main mercantile base in the county.

NATIVES FIGHT BACK

The truth, of course, was that the Irish hadn't really gone away; nor had the political ambitions of the O'Connors who were to play yet another military card before the walls of Athenry in 1316. A rather punitive invasion of Ireland by Edward Bruce from Scotland encouraged the O'Connor uprising, this time under Feidhlim, to engage with the Connacht colonists led by Sir William Liath de Burgo and Richard de Bermingham in bloody battle near Athenry.

Alas, the cream of native Connacht nobility fell in defeat on the fields of Athenry that day in 1316, and tradition has it that the walls of the nearby Bermingham town were reinforced with the spoils of battle.

TOWN of GALWAY GROWS

With the O'Connors rebuffed yet again, de Burgo might appeared absolute from the Shannon to the sea. However, despite this singular but impressive victory, more and more of the de Burgo tenantry deemed it prudent to move to Galway, a safer haven for ageing settlers and eager newcomers alike.

Of the latter, new merchant families bearing such names as Lynch (in time the most influential of the Tribes of Galway), Athy, Blake, Bodkin, Font, Joyce, Martin and Skerrett began to fill the burgher plots of the town. Ironically, while their burgage rent initially lined de Burgo pockets, within a few generations they would expel the descendants of the founding fathers from the town they knew so well!

DE BURGO LORDSHIPS

As the fourteenth century gathered pace, it was now the de Burgos' turn to feel the curse of western leadership weigh heavily on their shoulders. After Richard de Burgo died in 1242 a succession of de Burgos not only endeavoured to consolidate their rule of Connacht, but were also granted Ulster with Walter, Richard's son, becoming the 1st Earl of that province. However, Walter died, one suspects with a broken heart, in the castle at Galway in 1271 after failing to subdue yet another revolt, this time led by Hugh O'Connor.

His eldest son Richard became the 2nd Earl of Ulster but was better known as the 'Red Earl' due to his complexion. Under his command the embryonic town of Galway increased considerably in population and trade, and it is he who is associated with the aforementioned aisled-hall recently discovered in excavations under the present Custom House in the city.

However it would have been better if his son William, known as the 'Brown Earl', had confined himself to Connacht affairs, because the country, and in particular his tenant barons in Connacht, were shocked to learn of his assassination by servants in his castle at Carrickfergus in 1333. What happened next was a historical transformation which shook the English establishment in Ireland to the core.

DE BURGO REVOLT

Because William's only issue was a daughter, Elizabeth, who would shed all the de Burgo possessions on marriage into the hands of a stranger, a political revolution among the family ensued. Eventually this saw two of her cousins, both leaders of junior branches of the family, take complete control of de Burgo territories in Connacht, consisting mainly of the counties of Galway and Mayo today, contrary to hereditary law. Thanks to an agreement between them, Sir William, or Ulick of Annaghkeen (Castle) as he was more generally known, took possession of the various manorial lands of the present County Galway, while Edmund Albanach, who died in 1375, assumed control of those in County Mayo.

This drastic piece of land piracy was also contrary to English law, and to show that the English writ no longer applied to their newly acquired properties, both men declared independence from the Crown. As a consequence, they embraced the ancient laws of the Irish as well as their language and dress. In the process they became 'more Irish than the Irish themselves' as the de Burgo name changed eventually to Burke for those of the family who lived under the lordship of Ulick in County Galway, and to Bourke in County Mayo.

To demonstrate their Gaelic conversion even more, Ulick adopted the title of Mac (Son of) William Uachtar (Upper), with Edmund delighting under the title of Mac William Íochtar (Lower). Both titles honoured their father, Sir William Liath de Burgo, who founded the Abbey of St Francis outside the rising walls of Galway in 1296 and was buried in its grounds when he died in 1324. Ironically, the rather cruelly jettisoned

Elizabeth later married Lionel, Duke of Clarence, and from their union descended Edward IV.

By now, of course, the die was cast, and as the fourteenth and fifteenth centuries spanned their course the Burkes consolidated their extended families' grip on the confiscated lands of County Galway, free initially from any interference or pressures from an England occupied with its own internal political problems, compounded by the aftermath of the Black Death in 1348.

RESURGENCE OF IRISH CLANS

Consolidation came in various forms, not least the seeking of accommodation with native Irish clans whose dynastic ambitions were boosted by the lessening of relations between the Burkes and the Crown. Inter-clan marriages played a part in this process as when Annabella Burke married O'Brien, Earl of Thomond, thus concluding a strange but powerful alliance between former warring families.

These overtones, of course, saw various Irish clans endeavour to regain lost status by copying the new military stratagems of the occupiers. In this regard the arrival of the tower house on the Galway landscape was a welcome if less expensive option for colonist and Irish gentry alike, compared to the huge 'royal' castles at Roscommon and its Irish (O'Connor) counterpart at nearby Ballintubber.

ARRIVAL OF The TOWER HOUSE

Normally built of native limestone and rising up to 60 ft in height, these tower houses, initially modelled on the £10 towers of the Leinster Pale usually within walled courtyards, were a somewhat belated success when introduced into the Galway landscape in the fifteenth century— they remained in fashion up to the middle of the seventeenth century.

The Burkes led the way in tower house construction, accounting for most of these castles in County Galway as they endeavoured to build communication and defensive webs across the plains of Connacht. They also built the largest ones with those at Oranmore and Claregalway being prime examples, while Thoor Ballylee purchased by W. B. Yeats in 1917 for £35 is perhaps the most famous of their ancient castles.

IRISH TOWER HOUSES

The Irish clans also drew inspiration from these new, high-rise, and for the time, well-defended homes of their Burke masters, with for instance the Kellys building a tower house at Garbally. To the south the O'Heyne clan were associated with their kinsmen, the O'Shaughnessys, in the ownership of Dunguaire Castle, now a favourite tourist attraction at Kinvara, while the O'Shaughnessys were also very much associated with Fiddaun, Derryowen and Ardamullivan castles near Gort in South Galway.

To the west in Connemara the O'Flahertys also built tower houses, with the rather splendid six-storey example at Aughnanure near Oughterard acting as their spiritual home base, and now a much-visited tourist attraction after it was re-roofed in recent times.

As these great towers of stone began to rise towards the end of the fifteenth century, however, their lengthening shadows presaged unrest in a troubled Late Medieval period in County Galway. The powerful lordship of the Burkes was declining as local Gaelic chieftains sought greater independence in the running of their petty kingdoms. Even in the expanding seaport of Galway, Burke administration was under threat from the emerging power of its merchant families.

TOWN of GALWAY EXPANDS

Already various murage charters were granted to its citizens, allowing tolls to be collected on commodities such as fleeces, hides, salt, fish and wine, and the revenue collected financed the building of the town's defensive walls. Initially a gift from the de Burgos, murage charters took on a royal and consequently a more palatable flavour when the aforementioned Edward IV granted one to the town, the proceeds of which finally enclosed it with the necessary defensive walls. Later, Richard II granted a perpetual one in 1395, but even more exciting was his royal grant the following year which made the town a royal borough, allowing the citizens to elect their leader called a sovereign, replacing the portreeve appointed by the de Burgos.

MAYORAL TOWN

The ultimate goal was complete municipal independence, which finally arrived in 1484 when royal permission to elect its first mayor, Pyerse Lynch, was granted by Richard III to the town. Not surprisingly, an early edict issued by the new council saw the Burkes finally denied the right of lordship over the town they had founded and protected for over two centuries.

COLLEGIATE CHURCH of ST NICHOLAS

Important also was the change in the appointment process of the head of the town's parish church, St Nicholas's, founded in 1320. The growing importance and influence of Galway was also seen in the successful petition from its merchants to Pope Urban VI to change St Nicholas's to collegiate status, complete with warden and a college of eight vicars. More subtly this successful petition also saw the actual appointment of the town clergy being transferred into the hands of the newly elected Corporation, as Galway became a powerful city-state, free not only from Burke manorial administration, but also from Irish ecclesiastical rule from Knockmoy and Tuam.

INTERNATIONAL TRADE

'As proud as a Galway merchant' is an old saying which certainly describes the international attention the town, now a city in medieval terms, was getting as its trade with France, Italy, Spain and Britain increased. Wine, initially French but later Spanish, poured into its cellars beneath fine 'statelie buildings all built upon one plan' as its harbour facilities kept pace with the increasing trade.

There were exceptions to this 'one plan', however, as in time 12 new city mansions broke the stony skyline of 14 streets laid out in a grid pattern. Thus the regal homes of the merchant families drew foreign acclaim, of which only Lynch's Castle survives intact today, its much-embellished façade with coats of arms, merchant marks and exquisitely carved hood-mouldings remaining unsullied by later nineteenth-century plaster renderings.

The nearby Church of St Nicholas was enduring welcome growth pains as the merchant oligarchy, in thanksgiving for their growing fortunes, added greatly to its structure. As the fifteenth century drew to its close, the coming of the Dominicans to the western bank of the estuary in 1488 and the building of a monastery overlooking the little Claddagh fishing village, followed by the Augustinians a few years later (1504) to 'Forthill' on the south of the city walls, enhanced the increasing importance of the town. Little wonder then that a foreign merchant was heard to enquire in what part of Galway lay Ireland!

UNEASY PEACE

An uneasy peace lay across the lands of the Corrib in the growing vacuum created by the political revolt of the Burkes, as the fifteenth century drew to a close. Although still a power in terms of land tenure, thanks mainly to the control exercised from their main Loughrea manor and their many tower houses dotting the old manorial territories, pressure was mounting on the Burke dynasty, not least from within, as the family expanded into various branches, each vying for power.

Externally, agents of the Crown were seeking to establish central control yet again, while the main urban centre, the growing seaport of Galway, had actually rescinded local Burke authority with the establishment of a mayoralty system based on a biased merchant-based franchise. With local Gaelic chieftains on both sides of the Corrib also showing unrest, the territories of medieval Galway were a breeding ground of political dissent as medieval times slipped into history with the ebbing tide of fifteenth-century Ireland. Each passing year now seemed to herald a more alarming stop as our journey through time rushes towards the dawn of the Early Modern period, complete with its changes, which were to have a devastating effect on the medieval Gaelicised as well as Gaelic lordships of Connacht.

EARLY
5 MODERN
GALWAY

EARLY 15TH-CENTURY INSECURITY

The DAWN OF A NEW millennium, as experienced in recent times, is the cause of much celebration. One presumes this may have been the case also when the special half-millennium milestone signalled the start of the sixteenth century. Presumption is a frivolous assumption, however, because the political situation then was simply fraught with danger, a greater evil than inflation is today.

Political insecurity at any time is not to be welcomed; and as state factors impinged on the life of the simple herder, farmer and baker, the scene was not a happy one when scribes began to record the early 1500s in some detail. Initially, the political interests of three distinct parties shattered any hope of a centralised authority ensuring peace and prosperity for these western lands, with each group singing loudly from its own political hymn sheet.

The BURKES

The Burkes led the way, of course, when the main branch led by Ulick 'Fionn', known also as William Burke Uachter, greeted the start of the sixteenth century with vengeance in his heart. While the expulsion of the ancient de Burgos from the town of Galway was a sleight to be redressed, the capture of that thriving seaport in 1504 by William Burke, ably assisted by powerful southern allies, the O'Briens, McNamaras and O'Carrolls, suggested more than a local revolt, thus demanding a swift response from central authority.

It came when the Lord Deputy, the Earl of Kildare, aided by the O'Donnell and O'Kelly clans, met the insurgents on the slopes of a famous hill dominating the rolling farmlands seven miles north of Galway City. On 19 August 1504, in one of the bloodiest battles fought in Ireland, the Burkes and their allies were defeated, with both sides employing Scottish galloglaí mercenaries, famous for their proficiency in the use of the battleaxe. Since then, the battle site has been referred to as Knockdoe (the Hill of the Axes), where the ancient de Burgo dynasty finally foundered, never to be an independent power again. The Burkes, however, were not to be discounted from western power struggles of later times.

RICH MERCHANTS

As a consequence, the merchants of Galway, the second group exerting political power in the environs of these Corrib lands, rejoiced in their deliverance. In celebration of this great victory they commissioned the Earl of Kildare's coat of arms to be inscribed on the side façade of Lynch's Castle in Shop Street, where it can still be seen today.

Free at last to indulge their favourite passion of fair-wind trading, Galway's merchant classes saw the local quaysides welcome Spanish galleons, their holds filled with exotic commodities of wine, salt and spices. These sailing craft subsequently exited from Galway's busy harbour laden with hides, wool and fish, local harvests of land and sea. Not surprisingly, Galway rejoiced in being the third most important port in these islands, according to commentary at the time.

As often in such situations, rejoicing soon transformed itself into civic pride as Galway continued to grow internally with 'useful' public works such as street paving and a hospital dedicated to St Bridget in the east suburbs being provided, as well as much private building evident within its curtain walls. Town castles, in reality urban versions of tower houses erected by the Lynch, Blake and French families in particular, as well as many additions to the Church of St Nicholas, added greatly to the town's unique architecture, a source of wonder to the visitor and pride to the citizen.

Galway pride also manifested itself in the arbitrary choice of coats of arms by the merchant families, singularly done it seems without too much recourse to the heraldic authority of the time. Thus by the 1530s, there were ample signs that Galway was evolving into a powerful, independent city-state, happy to be safeguarded by the forces of a distant Crown but more than willing to plough its own economic furrow.

IRISH CHIEFTAINS

Independence was also very much on the political agenda of local Gaelic chieftains, the third agent in our political inventory as the six-teenth century saw its first quarter troubled by native unrest. The loyal citizens of Galway prayed (as recalled in a stone plaque said to have been displayed on the Great West Bridge, where O'Brien's Bridge is today) for deliverance from 'the ferocious O'Flahertys', ever a threat across the Corrib from the west.

To the south, O'Shaughnessy tower houses signalled the growing native restlessness, as did those of the O'Kellys and O'Maddens to the east.

CROWN CONTROL

Obviously it was time for the Crown or central authority to reactivate its claim of supremacy in the West. The perfect start was made with the Knockdoe victory reminding everyone that the Crown still retained more than a passing interest in its western territories. The key to overall supremacy, however, lay in the town of Galway itself, the growing power base of Connacht in political as well as economic matters. By the 1530s, however, the town's insular English authority and culture were being undermined.

GAILLIMH — TOWN OF T*h*e STRANGERS

Founded initially as a military and then an urban site to offer sanctuary to the early colonists, its very name of Galway, from the Gaelic Gaillimh (the Town of the Strangers) ensured, initially at least, that it was to be a settlement of foreign freemen to which no native need apply. At first security was all important and 'no O or Mac' was allowed to swagger down its streets, walk its defensive walls or dip a sail in the thriving harbour.

Alarmingly, from the point of view of the English establishment, how-ever, increased trading with the native hinterlands saw a diminution in the town's anti-Gaelic legislation and a gradual Irish influence begin to filter through its main gate. The accession of the Tudors to the English throne was timely, and its royal occupants soon put an end to such relaxations, as Galway came to play its part in international affairs. These affairs were already broadening into a growing American adven-ture, a gathering war with Spain, while nearer home the woes of Reformation were soon to occupy minds among Church establishments across the country.

The royal parchment of 1536 spelt it out, in which the words of Henry VIII were stern reminders for the citizens of Galway to return to their roots. Shaving their upper lips (which nowadays causes concern to some of the Early Galway Music Group) and practising with the English longbow were timely reminders to the young men of sixteenth-century Galway as to where their true loyalties should lie. Meanwhile the visit in 1536 of Lord Grey, the Lord Deputy, to Galway town, whose defences he greatly enhanced, emphasised changing fortunes for its citizens as well as those burdened by ambition outside its walls.

EARL O*f* CLANRICARDE

Of the latter perhaps Richard Óg Burke, brother of the defeated Ulick 'Fionn', best illustrates this notion of ambition when he usurped the title of MacWilliam Uachter. His grandnephew, Ulick na gCeann (of the Heads) Burke, having submitted like other Irish chieftains to Lord Grey in 1538 during his Munster visit, accompanied the Lord Deputy back to Connacht and was delighted to receive all of Richard Óg's territories taken by Grey in that year's campaign, which included the baronies of Loughrea, Athenry, Clare, Leitrim, Dunkellin and Kiltartan. There was more, of course, and for his loyalty Ulick na gCeann was made the 1st Earl of Clanricarde (the clan of Richard 'de Burgo') by Henry VIII in 1543. In effect the earl was given control in the king's name in what has been described as the surrender and re-grant system of the family's seized territories of County Galway, and was recompensed on a yearly basis for the de Burgo loss of revenue from the town of Galway itself, thus underpinning the town's local independence all the more. Seeing the advantages of the surrender and re-grant system, many other Irish chieftains such as the O'Flahertys, Kellys and Maddens also availed of this innovative way of gaining official control over their lands under the tenets of English common law rather than the old Gaelic system of land tenure and succession.

REFORMATION

By now Henry VIII had divorced Catherine of Aragon and as events unfolded, the Reformation initially had little effect on the religious affairs of Galway or its countryside. Mass was still celebrated in the Church of St Nicholas in Galway even after local signings of the Act of Supremacy demanded by the visiting Lord Grey. The dissolution of the monasteries, however, saw the three monastic properties of the Franciscans, the Augustinians and the Dominicans on the outskirts of Galway being confiscated, as happened also with those in the country areas. But life went on, with monks living locally and carrying on as best they could under the new and difficult circumstances. In Galway one finds many of the wealthy merchants still embellishing their favourite Church of St Nicholas during what must have been difficult times after its seizure in 1551.

The main changes at local level, however, were political when central control became a necessity in a world of changing alliances as the second half of the sixteenth century saw international affairs impact upon the politics of Connacht. Spain, long welcome participants in the trading affairs of Galway, was now becoming an enemy of England, and as a result fears were being raised about the security as well as the loyalties of the western town and its surrounding territories.

NEED FOR NATIONAL SECURITY

New initiatives were needed to increase national security which included the installation of government at provincial level to exercise strict control over re-granted local lordships. In Connacht Sir Edward Fitton was appointed President of the province in 1569, but even his ruthless methods of administration did not stop another western revolt, this time led by Ulick and John Burke, the sons of the Earl of Clanricarde, from ravaging the Galway countryside, razing Athenry and reducing the trade and status of the town of Galway to a ruinous state. However, with the defeat of a corresponding Munster rebellion and the eventual succession of Ulick as the 3rd Earl of Clanricarde, peace again descended and English rule gradually became the norm in a conflict-weary province.

Not surprisingly these internal alarms led to some important changes, which were to alter completely the physical and political status of the town and baronies of Galway. Athlone, adjacent to the forces of the Pale, became the headquarters of the new President of Connacht, a move which saw a stout stone bridge being built there in 1566 across the River Shannon by Sir Henry Sidney, the Lord Deputy, followed in 1577 by another bridge at Ballinasloe over the River Suck erected by Sir Nicholas Malby, who succeeded Fitton as President of Connacht. A military communication route between Galway and Dublin was now open and when, for the first time, 100 English troops were stationed in the western town in 1579, the independent status of Galway had come to an end.

COUNTY GALWAY FORMED

Two other sixteenth-century events need recording. When Sir John Perrot, the new Lord Deputy, visited Galway in 1584, he improved the administration processes under the presidency of Connacht by dividing the province into the six counties of Galway, Mayo, Roscommon, Sligo, Leitrim and Clare (the latter would return by its own request to Munster some years later). The county of Galway was in extent some 1,566,354 acres, the second largest in Ireland.

The way was now open in 1585 for the ultimate Composition of Connacht, which saw the final surrender of western lands to the Crown and their humiliating re-granting to subdued 'Lords, Chieftains and Freeholders' at a fixed fee. As the 1580s drew to a close, Elizabeth I, the new English monarch, had, thanks to her representatives, gained control over much of Ireland as a huge Spanish naval fleet sailed up the English Channel. In a few short weeks three of its storm-battered vessels would land on Galway shores with disastrous results.

SPANISH ARMADA

The year was 1588 as the Spanish Armada, thwarted in its invasion plans for England, set sail for home via Scotland and the west coast of Ireland. Much has been written about this ill-fated maritime venture, which saw the greatest storm of the century scatter the once proud fleet to the four winds off the west coast of Ireland. Inevitably three of these mighty sailing craft, still laden with troops, came ashore along the Connemara coastline.

The first of these, the *Falco Blanco Mediano*, ran aground on reefs off Freaghillaun Island in Ballynakill Bay near Clifden with much loss of life. Significantly, those who survived certainly did not enjoy traditional Irish hospitality. The same fate awaited those enticed ashore from the *Concepcion* at Mace Head off Carna, tempted, according to tradition, by fires lit by the local McDonogh clan under instructions from Tadgh na Buile (of the Anger) O'Flaherty, the local lord. Warned about the severe penalties for aiding Armada survivors, local coastal chieftains had no option but to turn over survivors to Richard Bingham, President of Connacht.

While those unfortunate survivors from these two ships were being transported to Galway, yet another Spanish vessel anchored off Barna and sent ashore some 70 of its personnel in search of provisions about the town of Galway, with which Spanish ships had traded so much wine just a short time previously. Sadly, the cannon atop the Spanish Arch bastion were trained in their direction now as war took precedence over commerce. The unfortunate pawns were quickly captured. They and the rest of the Spanish survivors were to pay a terrible price for seeking refuge in a land that might have given sanctuary.

Execution was all that the Lord Deputy, William FitzWilliam, could subsequently offer 300 of the terrified survivors on the slopes of the confiscated Augustinian monastery overlooking Lough Atalia. As the execution axes flashed in the midday sun, the greatest act of mass murder in Galway's history took place where Forthill Cemetery slumbers today.

A simple plaque erected on the east wall of the cemetery in 1988, with words in Spanish and Irish (there is no room for the language of the perpetrator!) record this chilling deed:

1588–1988
LA ORDEN DEL TERCIO VIEJO DEL MAR OCEANO,
A LOS MARINOS Y SOLDADOS DE LA GRAN ARMADA
AQUI PIADOSAMENTE ENTERRADOS POR EL PUEBLO DE GALWAY EN 1588
DECANCANSEN EN PAZ
22 de Junio de 1988
AR DHEIS DE GO RAIBH SIAD

As members of *La Orden Del Tercio Viejo Del Mar Oceano*, the oldest marine corps in the world, gathered on that unforgettable day in June 1988 in silver helmets and breastplates modelled on those worn in the sixteenth century, the final act in this terrible drama was enacted on the slopes of this quiet hill. The plaque they erected not only commemorated those executed on this hallowed spot, it also endorsed the dignified act of burial of the unfortunate victims carried out by the ordinary people of Galway, who were subsequently exonerated by papal decree of any blame for what happened in their town on that fateful day.

STRENGTHENING T*h*e DEFENCES

As the sixteenth century drew to a close, internal storm clouds were gathering again, and with the growing threat of a Spanish invasion very much a possibility, the loyal authorities in Galway and Athenry were again looking to strengthening their defences.

Athenry, recovering from the dreadful sacking of the town by the Earl of Clanricarde's sons earlier in the century, petitioned Queen Elizabeth for help in its recovery plans, which included seeking permission to invite more English artisans and tradesmen to settle in the town, the use of taxes to fortify the town walls and to grant Corporation status for 'the politique ordering of their affairs'. Seemingly the queen was receptive to their wishes and although no new charter 'passed the great seal', several new buildings and other improvements were made.

Galway also sought to strengthen its defences with the main attention being focused on the point of Ceann-na-Bhaile (now the Spanish Arch) where a bastion, complete with powerful cannon guarding the harbour and entrance from Galway Bay to the south, was constructed in the last decade of the sixteenth century.

RED HUGH O'DONNELL

The immediate danger came from the north, however, when the northern clans under Red Hugh O'Donnell were in open and powerful revolt in 1594, starting what has been described as the 'Nine Years' War'. In January 1596 his forces had reached the southern half of Connacht where they 'wasted, burned and destroyed almost the entire county of Galway'.

This simple statement masks the terror wrought by O'Donnell on the loyal settlements in the east of the county, as can be seen in the fate of Athenry, one of the most besieged urban settlements in the history of Ireland. On 15 January his forces overran its recently repaired walls with some ease, but could not take the misnamed King John's Castle. Instead, the entire town except for the castle, Dominican Abbey and parish church, was put to the torch.

Sadly, Athenry never recovered from this latest attack, being reduced in the nineteenth century to 'the state of an inconsiderable village'. Its fine array of town walls, still evident today, were never strong enough to defend the large area they encompassed. They stand as mute sentinels to ambition thwarted because the medieval population required to man them never materialised, unlike the nearby town of Galway, which was built on a smaller scale with much higher town walls backed up by appropriate water defences on three sides. Their strength was soon to be tested as O'Donnell and his army marched westwards as the smoke of Athenry billowed high behind them.

Despite peaceful overtones at first, Red Hugh was refused admission and so began the first siege of the town of Galway in its troubled history. Most of the eastern suburbs were put to the torch by the enraged northern troops, who gathered on the aforementioned Forthill for their initial thrust at the town defences. They never got into their stride, however, as a powerful cannonade from the town guns spread terror and confusion among their ranks. An armed sortie made by the town defenders at that precise moment saw O'Donnell and his followers break off the engagement. Heading northwards, they burnt the remaining east suburbs including St Bridget's Hospital and Church in that part of Bohermore which is now Prospect Hill.

Victory for the town of Galway was just a temporary respite, however, because war clouds were gathering elsewhere. The revolt in the north led by the O'Donnells and O'Neills was gathering even more momentum, while the threat of a Spanish invasion seemed imminent as the sixteenth century came to a close.

It was obvious as the new century dawned that Galway, the main maritime gateway to Connacht, needed further fortification, and a new citadel guarding the eastern approaches to the town as well as the harbour was a desired option. To emphasise this need, the Spanish made a landing at Kinsale and after their defeat there on Christmas Eve 1601 in a famous battle, building a citadel or strong fort either within or outside the town walls of Galway became a necessity in case they returned to Ireland.

DÓNAL O'SULLIVAN BEARE

This became all the more imperative because there was alarm in the eastern end of the county, when at the end of 1602, Dónal Cam O'Sullivan Beare with 400 troops and 600 non-combatants set off from Glengarriff in West Cork to link up with Hugh O'Neill in Ulster. Fighting against English forces still fresh from their victory in Kinsale, he eventually crossed the Shannon near Portumna and in the first Battle of Aughrim on 9 January 1603 he defeated a formidable force of five companies of foot and two of horse, assisted by native O'Kellys and Maddens, before heading northwards into Roscommon via Ballygar, Mount Mary, Glinsk and Ballymoe, a march much commemorated in recent times in these areas. Then, of course, it underlined the need for further defensive measures to be taken, especially in Galway City, open to an invasion from the sea by the Spanish who knew the sea route only too well.

FIRST MAPS of GALWAY CITY

As early as 1583 two maps of Galway City (then a town) had been provided in preparation for the building of a suitable bastion to provide protection for the harbour area. The first of these was drawn up by Barnaby Gooche, Provost-Marshal of Connacht, which gives a fascinating early glimpse of Galway towards the end of the sixteenth century. Compiled to be viewed by military commanders at a round table, the map depicts a fully walled city, with eight crenellated towers, three of which are over gateways, the main one classed as a barbican facing the major land threat from the east at today's Williamsgate Street. Another was erected over the Great West Bridge crossing the River Corrib in 1442, and the final one was situated at the junction of present-day Mary Street and Abbeygate Street Upper, leading to the Abbey of St Francis on St Stephen's Island. Across the river is indicated 'O'Flaherty Country', an ever-present threat from the dispossessed O'Flahertys, while a space for the new citadel was marked beside the extended wall bastion now known as the Spanish Arch. The other map, credited to John Brown and compiled some weeks later, only purports to show the actual town wall with its fortifications without reference to streets or internal buildings.

Because Ireland was seen as 'a fair step into England' and Galway was noted as 'a Spanish town', the need to further fortify the latter was all the more pressing, resulting in another map being made, this time by the brother of the Lord Deputy FitzWilliam in 1592 showing the complete 'Sircute of the Town of Gallaway' which, unlike the previous two, showed the outlying topography of the town including the estuary, Mutton Island, and also the hilly terrain surrounding the town. Here for the first time, the flaw in the defensive arrangements of the town were noted, because it was dominated by hills on either side of the river, from which military fire could be directed into the town.

Red Hugh O'Donnell illustrated the most obvious of these when he took Forthill, next to the harbour, prior to his undignified retreat in 1596. As 1599 drew to a close, a surprise victory by his forces over those of the Crown under Clifford in the Curlew Mountains, following a more famous Irish one at the Yellow Ford in Ulster in 1598, saw most of Connacht rise up in revolt including the remnants of the O'Connors as well as Theobald Burke. The Earl of Clanricarde remained loyal, but with only some 800 men at his disposal he offered little threat to the resurgent Irish.

FORTHILL FORT

With the arrival of Lord Mountjoy, the Lord Deputy, the town of Galway was put on a war alert in 1600 and the building of the long-promised citadel or fort on Forthill (thus its name) began. In 1603 Sir Thomas Rotheram was appointed governor over town and fort. He commanded the fort for 33 years and even became Mayor of Galway in 1612, the first 'outsider' to achieve such a distinction in 170 years.

Built to protect the town of Galway and thus maintain the English presence in the West, this massive fort at Forthill, whose earthen ramparts can still be seen as one climbs the path in the present-day cemetery, in time became the town's Nemesis. Initially it fulfilled all its objectives. Even in an unfinished state its towering presence underlined the English intent of final domination in the Connacht realm, and as Mountjoy arrived in Athlone in December 1602 all the major western chieftains, which included the O'Flahertys but not the O'Rourkes, came to it to submit.

Again there was a Galway connection here, because with the death of Red Hugh O'Donnell, poisoned by Galway merchant and Crown spy, James Blake, in Spain in September of that year, the backbone of the Irish rebellion was broken. When Spain ended its 100 years of conflict with England in 1603, O'Neill finally submitted, followed shortly afterwards by O'Rourke. The fact that Queen Elizabeth died just then also, was immaterial to the Irish cause.

In the Connacht context, the rising military power of the English Crown, as evident in the construction of the citadel in Galway, showed the pivotal part the town was playing in the final acquiescence of its rebellious clans. The town had paid a heavy price, however, as its long-developed independence was much diminished by the permanent military presence. Its trade also suffered under the wartime trading restrictions. With increasing pressure for Church reform as the military alarm receded, it faced an even greater dilemma—loyalty to the Crown or continued allegiance to the Catholic religion was a challenge now to be faced not only by the population of County Galway but Ireland as a whole.

With most of the rural countryside as ever resentful of English authority, no matter how well administered, it now became the turn of the loyal towns to revolt against the growing religious intolerance of the Crown manifested through its administrators, especially in the aftermath of the Flight of the Earls in 1607, despite the fact that the new occupant of the throne, James, was a son of the Catholic Mary Stuart, Queen of Scots. All through his reign his policy of enforcing a Protestant regime on town and county finally broke down the barrier between the two sections—in Galway it simply meant that O's and Mac's were now *personae gratae* within its walls as the town began to prosper yet again from its revitalised overseas trade.

PRESIDENT of CONNACHT

Changes of note during this period saw Richard, Earl of Clanricarde, become Lord President of Connacht, while in 1610 a new royal charter saw the town of Galway become officially 'the County of the Town of Galway', enlarged to two miles, with the confiscated Franciscan Abbey, although inside the new boundary area, acting as the courthouse of the county itself.

The new 'County of the Town of Galway' was governed by a mayor and two sheriffs, with the former honoured from then on by having a magnificent municipal sword borne before him on ceremonial occasions. This huge silver sword and a subsequent eighteenth-century mace are displayed in City Hall today—both are still used on important municipal occasions, underlining the city's rich heritage in more ways than one.

COUNTY GALWAY DEFINED

The boundaries of County Galway were officially set in 1607 as being over 60 miles on an east/west axis from the Shannon to beyond

'Bunowne in Iar-Chonnacht' and in breadth from the Shannon to near Claremorris in Mayo, a distance of 37 miles 'or thereabouts'. Galway was now seen to be a vast county, with the growing promise of a commercial hub in the town of the same name. A small but professional military corps guarded its citadel as well as the town walls, and an auxiliary body of troops under the presidency of the Clanricardes was based in the county area itself.

SPEED'S MAP Of GALWAY, 1610

Happily, a new map by John Speed in 1610 shows the first proper perspective of the growing town of Galway, complete with sailing craft at anchor between the Spanish Arch bastion and the well-defended West Bridge. It was a place to welcome the various Crown dignitaries who regularly visited this important base of English power in the far west of Ireland. One of these was Sir Oliver St John who in 1614 wrote about his visit:

> The town is small, but has fair and stately buildings. The fronts of the houses (towards the streets) are all of hewed stone up to the top, garnished with fair battlements in a uniform course, as if the whole town had been built upon one model. The merchants are rich, and great adventurers at sea. Their commonalty is composed of the descendants of the ancient English founders of the town, and rarely admit any new English to have freedom or education among them, and never any of the Irish. They keep good hospitality and are kind to strangers; and in their manner of entertainment and in fashioning and apparelling themselves and their wives, they preserve most the ancient manner and state, as much as any town that ever I saw. The town is built upon a rock, environed almost with the sea and the river, compassed with a strong wall and good defences, after the ancient manner, and such as with a reasonable garrison may defend itself against an enemy.

Of interest here is the comment on the rich merchants who were also 'great adventurers at sea'. These merchant adventurers, bearing the family names of Lynch, Kirwan, Blake and Skerrett in particular, found richness in both the import and export business alike.

GROWTH Of INTERNATIONAL TRADE

In the first half of the seventeenth century, perhaps the golden era of mercantile endeavour for these merchant families soon to be classed as the 'Tribes of Galway', their chief import commodities consisted of wine (initially from France and Italy, but Spanish wine was favoured in later times), iron, salt, manufactured items including cloth, as well as spices and silks, the luxuries of the time.

Depots were set up overseas in the various countries involved as well as internally in Ireland such as in Athboy in County Meath to service the purchase and transport of these commodities. Meanwhile external Galway trading establishments overseas in the West Indies, Spain, Portugal and France in particular, were also involved in the town's export market which saw vast amounts of hides/leather, wool, fish, tallow, cattle, grain and timber make their way out beyond Mutton Island as brave sea captains (including Christopher Columbus on his voyage between Bristol and Iceland in 1477) ploughed their frail vessels into waves fashioned in Brazil.

Integral with this huge surge in business activity carried on by a population estimated at over 5,000 in the early decades of the seventeenth century, was the strict control exercised by Galway Corporation through murage or taxes imposed on trading transactions as well as regulations imposed to keep the markets stable. In times of shortage, restrictions on the export of such items were imposed, while rules as to whom should be served first in the town's seven markets seem archaic to modern eyes.

Each market day, as the seventeenth century progressed, more and more native produce from ever-extending surrounding areas entered Galway, with an increase in the area of such heavy goods as cattle and grain coming from an unlikely source.

TRIBES MOVE TO COUNTRYSIDE FROM GALWAY

By then many of the tribal families had gained possession of more and more real estate in County Galway as a result of the Clanricarde Burkes seeing economic as well as political survival in toeing the English line, unlike their fellow insurgents in Munster and Ulster. Continuous aggression by the native Irish in those provinces resulted in vast plantations taking place, with the inevitable forfeiture of life and land for those involved.

Encouraged by this turn of events, and with the need for legal expertise in the Compositions involving the grant and re-grant systems imposed by succeeding monarchs, a new avenue of advancement opened for some of the young and talented members of the tribal families of Galway. There was a need for legal proficiency in dealing with complex land titles and, as a result, the English Inns of Court beckoned for those young Galway men in particular whose families, thanks to international mercantile intercourse, had the means to send them overseas to train as lawyers.

Thus in the mostly peaceful times of the first quarter of the seventeenth century, learned sons of Galway merchants such as Patrick D'Arcy, the most famous Galway lawyer, were active in addressing the problems of defective titles in numerous land tenure applications, not only from harassed native chieftains and their tenants, but also from English Protestant landowners in Connacht and elsewhere who were also eager to avail of their services. In the case of the former, settlements for services rendered were often made in land grants to these merchant families, who also claimed land as security on money loaned. Gradually the merchant tribes of Galway expanded into land management not just in County Galway itself but even further northwards into Mayo and Sligo. In time, the new Catholic landlord elite including the Blakes, the Brownes and the Lynchs in particular owned 222,910 acres in County Galway alone.

DIFFICULTIES ON The RELIGIOUS FRONT

Problems also existed on the religious front. Despite the imposition of the reformed liturgy, especially towards the end of the seventeenth century, when Catholic worship in all its forms was curtailed, many of the lower ranks of the population continued to show devotion to the old faith secretly in private homes but sometimes in the open when the opportunity arose. The Oath of Supremacy acknowledging the King as head of the Church was still mandatory, and this often led to confront-ations resulting, for example, in the dismissal of four Galway mayors between 1610 and 1632. The arrival of counter-reformation influences from abroad kept the religious pot boiling—soon it would boil over and become part of a national uprising, which would bring catastrophic ·results to town and county.

ROYAL CLAIMS TO CONNACHT

On the political front also, things got progressively worse after Thomas Wentworth, Lord Deputy, landed in Ireland. Soon afterwards, in 1635, in pursuit of his goal of financing Charles I's continental intrigues, he again claimed Connacht for the King and appointed Commissioners of Plantation before whom local juries were compelled to ensure the claim. Not surprisingly Leitrim, Sligo, Roscommon and Mayo juries, under pressure, 'found the king's title without scruple'.

However when Wentworth and his political 'posse' came to Galway, according to James Hardiman in his *History of Galway*, published in 1820:

> . . . *their progress was stopped, and this arbitrary measure met with the most determined and effectual opposition from the gentlemen of the county, whose independent spirit, strict adherence to truth and justice, and conscientious discharge of their duty, on this occasion deserve to be for ever commemorated.*

For their stand, the sheriff, Martin D'Arcy of Kiltullagh near Athenry, and the appointed jury were immediately arrested and brought to Dublin Castle from Portumna, the seat of the jury sitting. For their bravery they were heavily fined, imprisoned and suffered severe treatment, which included such niceties as being 'pillored, with loss of ears and bored through the tongue'. As a consequence, Martin D'Arcy died in prison and only with the intervention of the Earl of Clanricarde were the fines reduced and the unfortunate jury released. Not surprisingly, when two new juries were appointed to account for the county of Galway and also for the town and its county in 1637, they found for the Crown. As a result of such defiance, both counties were planted at a higher rate, with the unfortunate landowners losing a half of their properties compared to a quarter for the other Connacht counties.

Fear, like death, is the great leveller among the people, uniting them in mind and purpose against the perceived threat. As a result of the aforementioned pressures on property and faith, a gradual uniting of the goals and aspirations of the majority of the once loyal inhabitants of the town of Galway with those of the Gaels without commenced.

LYNCH SCHOOL — HOTBED OF IRISH SCHOLARSHIP

This sea change in attitude was nourished by the gradual assimilation of the classical curriculum of the free school founded in Galway town in 1580 into one catering for the growing nationalist outlook of the populace in general. Irish language and culture figured greatly in the curriculum when Alexander Lynch became master and by 1608 it is said there were 1,200 pupils seeking education in the town which in effect, for a brief time, became the Gaelic heart of Ireland.

Closed in 1615 because Lynch would not conform to the established religion, the school reopened and by 1627 it had embarked on an even more nationalistic crusade, which led to the development of fine scholarship in Irish language, history and antiquities. Well-known academics associated with this venture included such luminaries of the time as Dr John and James Lynch as well as Roderic O'Flaherty who retired from Moycullen to Parke near Spiddal and went on to write such famous tracts as *Iar-Chonnacht* and *Ogygia*.

A contemporary of this great Gaelic Renaissance in Galway was Sligo's Duald Mac Firbus, the last of the famous genealogists of the O'Dowd clan, who came to Galway during these heady days of the 1640s and completed his most important work, the celebrated *Book of Genealogies*, in the expanded library attached to the Church of St Nicholas, before war brought ruin in its wake. The year was 1651 when hostilities broke out in Galway, but the truth was it had being brewing for a long time before that.

GALWAY'S OWN CIVIL WAR

The seeds of Galway's mini civil war had already been sown when Sir Francis Willoughby took command of the great citadel, then known as St Augustine's Fort, at Forthill in 1636 from Sir Thomas Rotheram. Although a smaller fortification was built to the west of the Great West Bridge in 1625, where the Galway Arms bar is today on the corner of Dominick Street, the Forthill citadel was the real centre of English military domination of the town, and ultimately the county, since its completion in 1603. Built primarily to protect Galway from Spanish invasion, it became a symbol of the growing power of the Parliamentarian campaign against the authority of the King before a sudden change of events in 1641 saw its role eventually reversed in a most spectacular manner.

On 23 October of that year one of the last major insurrections by the Catholics commenced in Ireland, a struggle which was to last nearly 11 years and saw victory eventually go to the new Parliamentarian army under Oliver Cromwell, thus leading to the total demise of the Catholic cause. The new year, 1642, saw the insurgents establish their own government in Kilkenny, known as the Supreme Council of the Irish Catholic Confederation, in which the Connacht interest was underlined by the appointment of Colonel John Burke as the supreme commander in the western province.

Caught in the middle of this religious struggle for supremacy was the Earl of Clanricarde, who was appointed governor of the town and county of Galway and who tried on numerous occasions to mediate between the warring factions in the Galway sphere of operations. His efforts at conciliation were becoming frustrated, however, as he became more and more isolated in the gathering struggle between the followers of the Puritan-led parliament and the Irish royalists. Locally the Earl tried to mediate between the adherents of the Confederation of Kilkenny who were at odds initially with the loyal followers of the Crown in the town of Galway. That the revolt was gaining ground in County Galway was made evident when the Archbishop of Tuam deserted his castle and Murchadh na dTua O'Flaherty captured Clanricarde's castle at Aughnanure near Oughterard.

FORTHILL FALLS

The local issue was solved in 1643 when the garrison at Forthill, now seen to be firmly on the side of the Parliamentarians under Willoughby, surrendered to the combined forces commanded by Colonel Burke, despite the efforts of the Earl of Clanricarde to mediate and to keep it supplied with provisions and ammunition. The Earl's forces of some 700 foot and 200 horse had garrisoned his castles at Oranmore, Claregalway and nearer the town at Terryland, to no avail, as the superior forces of Col Burke, backed up the townspeople and some 1,400 men who arrived earlier from Connemara, successfully laid siege to Forthill.

Willoughby put up stout resistance, helped by Parliamentarian naval power including a fleet of 17 ships under the command of Lord Alexander Forbes which arrived in Galway Bay on 7 August 1642. Units from this fleet landed at the Dominican Church in the Claddagh on the western shores of the Corrib estuary, and from its hallowed grounds bombarded the town in an attempt to subdue the growing rebellion, but without success. Angry at his failure to save Willoughby and his citadel force from 'Popish capture', Forbes caused his men to deface the Claddagh church and desecrate the graves of those interred in its grounds.

That town and county were consequently as one in the fight for religious freedom can be seen in the number of prominent townspeople including clergy who participated in the capture of the hated fort in 1643, backed up by such country gentlemen as the Berminghams from Athenry, the Kellys of Gallagh, Aughrim and Mullaghmore, and Sir Valentine Blake and Sir Roebuck Lynch, both with connections with the town. Of particular interest were the numbers of the Burke family who, despite the exhortations to peaceful means of their kin, the Earl of Clanricarde, took up arms for the Catholic cause. They included Sir Ulick Burke, Hurbert Burke of Donamon, Redmond Burke of Kilcornan, Richard Burke of Derrymacloghny and Thomas Burke of Anbally. With the relief of the town of Galway, only Loughrea and Portumna in the possession of the Earl of Clanricarde lay outside the influence of the Confederation of Kilkenny.

RELIGIOUS FREEDOM AGAIN

With victory achieved over the local Parliamentarian outpost in the west, the town of Galway quickly rejoiced in its new-found religious freedom, with Catholic worship again in vogue in the various abbeys, and also with great joy and celebrations in the ancient Church of St Nicholas itself. The fort on Forthill was soon demolished, except for the former Augustinian church building which had been utilised as a barracks within the ramparts of the fort and which was now handed back to the Augustinians. They would reoccupy it for only two years, however, before the reality of the town's precarious position became clear.

With Charles now in serious conflict with his parliament, the town of Galway still professed loyalty to the troubled monarch. Thus, it sided with the Confederation, which ceased hostilities in the prevailing circumstances with Charles's followers in Ireland. However, various clergy including Rinuccini, Papal Nuncio to the Confederation, preached against it and advocated a complete separation between Ireland and England.

This troubled cleric eventually came to Galway, where he caused much dissension among the local clergy and instigated rioting among the populace, before the Earl of Clanricarde laid siege to the town in a successful attempt to stop what could have been a serious rebellion from gaining momentum. As a disillusioned Rinuccini boarded the *San Pedro* anchored off Long Walk and sailed away, he left behind a town and country preparing to face the growth of Parliamentarian might, already a *fait accompli* with the execution of Charles I in 1649. Ironically, one of his reputed executioners, Peter Stubbers, was given a rather special piece of property in Galway as payment for his services, which now rejoices in the title of The King's Head, one of the city's most popular pubs.

PARLIAMENTARIAN THREAT

Aware that it was only a matter of time before the siege drums would sound again, preparations were made between 1645 and 1649 to meet the Parliamentarian threat. In Galway massive bastions were erected on the eastern curtain wall facing Eyre Square, while other sections of the town wall were also strengthened. The town's ordnance was also added to with a supply of 12 powerful cannon purchased by the Corporation from France, while the old Augustinian Church on Forthill and the Dominican Church on the Claddagh hill were demolished in case they offered artillery base facilities to attacking forces. Amid these military preparations a terrible plague struck the town in 1649, during which over 3,500 people died within its walls—an ominous portent of what was to come. That fear became even greater with reported massacres of civilians by the Parliamentarian forces of Oliver Cromwell, as his new-age army of Ironsides marched from town to town across the country after coming ashore in Dublin in August 1649. They quickly took Athlone, Portumna and Killaloe on their relentless push westwards, despite the efforts of Clanricarde and his Connacht Confederate allies.

SIEGE Of GALWAY

In July 1651 the warm sun glistened on the helmets of the feared 'roundheads' as they gathered in force on the slopes of Prospect Hill above the town of Galway and spread a ring of steel and siege works from Lough Atalia to the River Corrib, taking Terryland Castle as well as those at Claregalway and Oranmore on the way.

With battle lines drawn up, the Parliamentarians under Sir Charles Coote and the town defence forces under the command of Preston frequently clashed, and a long siege lasting nine months ensued after various truce offers were turned down by both sides.

With no relief prospects coming from the east due to the numerous siege lines and forts erected by Coote, very little succour coming from the west of the county, and no word of help from the Duke of Lorraine in France, the town of Galway finally succumbed to defeat, despite the protestations of most of the clergy and the bulk of the common people. After nine months of siege the town's 'fathers' surrendered on 3 April 1652.

PEACE TREATY BROKEN

Although a peace treaty was signed by both warring parties, one which offered quite reasonable terms to the citizens of Galway, these same terms were quickly broken by the victors who proceeded to turn a once powerful Catholic city-state into a nondescript Protestant town. Initially ordered to pay in cash one-third of their stated properties as war reparations, followed by an illegal levy of £400 collected monthly, eventually most of the citizens were ordered out of the town to make way for planters from the cities of Gloucester and Liverpool, active allies of the Parliamentarian adventurers in their military campaigns.

Before that, a thousand unfortunate captives taken from town and county by Col Peter Stubbers, who was appointed governor and eventually mayor of Galway in 1654, were sent overseas to such places as the West Indies as slaves, followed by 50 clergymen who were first imprisoned on Inishboffin in a huge star-shaped fort erected by the Cromwellians. Worse was to follow as many of the distraught citizens of Galway were banished to the winter countryside surrounding their town, where ditches rapidly filled with their freezing bodies, as the plague again revisited the region, claiming thousands in its deathly grasp.

The town itself suffered no better. The once proud city-state experienced the worst moments in its long history as a contemporary report pointed out:

> *You may see whole families destroyed and streets not having six families, and that soldiers or poor beggars that ought to content themselves with one cellar, had great houses to live in till they burnt all the lofts and wainscots and partitions thereof, and then remove to another house till they made an end of all the town, and left them full of excrements and filth, that it was poison to enter into any of the said houses, formerly fit to lodge kings or princes.*

Despite such degradation of the once fine buildings, the new city rulers including Col Peter Stubbers, the Meyricks (after whom Meyrick Square, now Eyre Square was named) and the Eyres (including Edward who presented the square and civic mace to the city in 1710) were soon involved in erecting two powerful citadels at both major entry gates to the town—at the Great West Bridge (O'Brien's Bridge) and at the eastern entrance where the Edward Square Shopping Centre is today. From the Parliamentarian point of view, however, all this came to nought on the Restoration of Charles II in 1660.

RESTORATION ACTS

With a new king on the throne again, many of those new Protestant landowners both in the town and county, who were 'distinguished for the violence of their principles', suddenly disappeared, especially when Charles II ordered some restoration of property to his faithful followers in the town of Galway. Because of this declaration, many of the dispossessed Catholic merchants sought the restoration of their properties such as Robert Martin of Ross who demanded that his mansion house be returned to him by Edward Eyre, the Town Recorder. When the lords justices directed in favour of the latter, it became clear that the status quo had hardly changed at all.

In the countryside things were hardly different, with most of the merchant landowners losing some of their lands or were transplanted to smaller holdings elsewhere. Perhaps through their new-found legal expertise some merchant families actually increased their holdings, such as the Frenches of Monivea and various members of the Browne, Kirwan and Lynch families. Smaller grants, some 580 in all, were made to lesser families including Roderic O'Flaherty, but the main talking points were the restoration of Richard Burke, the 6th Earl of Clanricarde, to his vast estates in East Galway and the ousting of the O'Flahertys in Connemara in favour of the Martins of Galway.

The reneging on his initial promise to return town property to the townspeople of Galway was compounded even further when the King granted all the former Corporation lands and market dues to Elizabeth Hamilton, the widow of James Hamilton, one of the grooms of his bedchamber! This added insult to injury, and the great exodus of members of the merchant oligarchy to safer and more lucrative climes, as well as to their country estates, had already begun.

Those who remained tried to reinvigorate the old trade routes to the Continent, which had seen Galway reach its true mercantile potential before the Parliamentarian siege of the town. Ironically, this greatness was clearly depicted in the famous pictorial map of Galway, said to have been drawn up in 1651 to induce the Duke of Lorraine to finance the King's army, but more likely completed in the reign of Charles II to underline the town's everlasting fidelity to the royal cause.

NEW CIVIL WAR

With the accession of James II, Charles II's Catholic brother, the Duke of York, to the throne in 1685, the ingredients for a new civil war were already beginning to mix when James was forced to flee to France because of his promotion of the Catholic ethos in a Protestant England. When Dutchman, William, Prince of Orange, was welcomed to the throne by the English establishment, it was only a matter of time before the two would meet in the deadly anger of military engagement. It was at the little village of Aughrim in County Galway on 12 July 1691 that the main battle was fought, while the more famous Battle of the Boyne was only a skirmish by comparison.

It had all started so well for Catholic Galway with the accession of James II, who bestowed his royal favour and protection on the town which had stood so steadfastly for the old religion and loyal to the royal cause in the most trying of times. In August 1686 James Kirwan (later of Castlehacket near Tuam) became the first Catholic mayor of Galway for over a quarter of a century, and a Catholic Corporation was recalled, as well as a warden and vicars installed in the Church of St Nicholas. On the county scene four major infantry regiments were raised under the command of Lord Bophin, the Earl of Clanricarde, Lord Galway and Dominick Browne from Castlemagarrett.

When James came to Ireland, Galway saw many of its former Catholic citizens back in possession of their properties, and 'the Protestant inhabitants were afterwards removed by the governor to the west suburbs, for the better security of the town'. Most significant of all, Mass began to be openly celebrated again in the old churches and abbeys throughout the town and county.

Typical of these happy reunions was that which occurred in the beautiful friary of Ross Errilly outside Headford. Jim McHugh in his history of this famous abbey by the Black River described what happened:

> The friars of Ross then availed themselves of the opportunity to repair the ravages done to their friary. Altars were re-erected, tombs closed and sealed, woodwork re-fixed, and the whole house again made habitable, so that the friars returned to their chancel-stalls and once more Ross re-echoed to the joyous 'Te Deum' by the Franciscans. . . . Complete freedom returned for the brief reign of the Catholic James II, and there exists a record, which tells that the assembled friars of Ross, in 1687, prayed there for the welfare of James and his queen.

BATTLE Of AUGHRIM

Their prayers were in vain. The threatened civil war between the two kings finally began to spill mainly Irish blood in fierce battles from Derry to the Boyne, and from the bridge at Athlone to the green slopes of Aughrim, where the two royal armies finally met in the most savage battle fought in Ireland. The general consensus suggests that upwards of 6,000 men were killed in this terrible engagement on that fateful day of 12 July 1691, as Catholic Ireland finally crumbled before the might of Williamite forces commanded by General Ginkel.

As the varied components of the shattered Jacobite army fled the field, leaving their French commander St Ruth headless on the blood-spattered slopes of Aughrim, the dull cannonading sounds of that terrible action had already reached the refugee-packed streets of Galway nearly 40 miles away. Here, frantic efforts were made to install extra defence lines as the vanguard of the Williamites drew ever closer, with the main body reaching Athenry by 18 July.

WILLIAMITE SIEGE Of GALWAY

As the main body of troops, some 14,000 infantry, began their westward march on the following morning, dissension was already evident among the Galway defenders, mainly under French command and consisting of only seven regiments of troops and a few troops of horse, as to whether they should defend the town or surrender. However, with the burning of Terryland Castle upstream of the town by French defenders at the approach of the Williamites, the die was cast, and for nearly a week the sound of cannonading echoed across the huge, reinforced limestone walls guarding the town's eastern quarters. With the besiegers success-fully crossing the River Corrib at Menlo in specially constructed tin boats, and the capture of the strategic Forthill position, the town had no option but to surrender on 21 July.

Again truce articles were signed, which saw Lord Dillon and some 2,500 troops march out of Galway for Limerick, which held out for another three months before Catholic opposition to the Protestant throne finally ended. Galway's Catholics under 16 articles of capitulation were given a free pardon, allowed to possess their estates and even carry arms. Significantly, Catholic clergy were to be unmolested 'in the private exercise of their religion'.

PENAL LAWS

However, the fate of the Catholics in Galway town and county was sealed by the dangers they posed to the establishment. Easily outnumbering those in authority, they looked on in dismay as various laws were passed by parliament gradually annulling the guarantees given in the 1691 surrender terms, thus ensuring Protestant ascendancy in Galway in terms of government, religion, trade and land tenure. While the dreaded Anti-Catholic Penal Laws came into place across the entire country from 1695, specific Acts were promulgated with a special Galway intent, such as the 1703 edict prohibiting Catholics from purchasing or renting property in the town, while another in 1717, known simply as 'The Galway Act', ensured Protestant control of Galway Corporation leading to the demise of the original merchant oligarchy. The main consequence of these Acts was a slowing down of the town's commerce and trade during the eighteenth century.

In the countryside it was even worse, where under the Penal Laws land tenure by Catholics was forbidden, with estates forfeited, and many of the old 'English' families such as the Clanricarde Burkes, Berminghams, Martins and Frenches converted to Protestantism, although initially after Aughrim some 78 representatives of the Catholic gentry retained their properties.

While 59 per cent of landownership in Ireland in 1641 was in Catholic hands, by 1703, due to the Penal Laws and forfeiture after the Williamite Wars it had fallen to 14 per cent. In many cases the eldest son of the landed estate conformed (the Earl of Clanricarde, Lord Bophin, bargained for his estates by having his two eldest sons reared in the Protestant faith, thus holding on to his family estate) as the era of the Ascendancy and the Teach Mór (Big House) dawned, leaving the voice of the smaller Catholic landlord muted.

RELIGIOUS DISCRIMINATION

The Penal Laws were even more pernicious against the Catholic religion itself. In 1691 the English Parliament passed a bill that no one could sit in the Irish Parliament without taking the Oath of Supremacy. In 1697 another bill sought the listing of all Catholic clergy in the country, which noted 68 secular, 60 regular clergy and one bishop, Dr Murtagh Donnellan of Clonfert, in the Galway excise district alone. All were required to depart the country by 1 May 1698, of which 190 from the Connacht region left Galway port in that year. Many chose to stay with their flocks, however, and so the terrible era of the 'priest hunter', Mass rock and Mass house, as well as hedge schools commenced.

As the eighteenth century opened, there were constant proclamations and cases of priest-hunting in the Galway region, with spies everywhere. With £100 being offered for the 'taking' of a bishop, not surprisingly Dr Donnellan was captured, but he was rescued 'in her Majesty's highway in the County of Galway by a great multitude of persons, 300 in number, some whereof were mounted on good horses and well armed . . .' Obviously the people of the county were not to be intimidated, and the legends of the Mass rock commenced, when fugitive priests celebrated the mystery of the Eucharist on large boulders in lonely glens and wooded dells.

From Glassillaun in the parish of Ballynakill in Connemara, to Gort na hAltóra in Ballybrit Racecourse in Galway City right on to over 40 Mass houses recorded in the parishes of Clonfert, the spirit of the old faith was very much alive. Catholic education was also proscribed, which led to numerous hedge schools being set up throughout the county, with 13 reported in the diocese of Clonfert alone.

UNFAIR LAND TENURE

The main complaint, however, among the common folk of the countryside was that they had become slaves in the land of Ireland. Not able to own any property of their own, vast numbers of them clustered together as tenants of unsympathetic Protestant landlords in humble little clachans (villages) without church, school or inn. Work was their only lot, and while the potato was a godsend, allowing families to grow in number, the rundale system they operated was in time bound to fail. The great big boundary walls still to be seen running up the sides of Connemara mountains show how jealously they guarded their leased land from each other, with faction fights often the outcome at fairs and other gatherings.

Meanwhile, the landlords of County Galway lived in the lap of luxury provided by the sweat of tenants and servants as the eighteenth century drew to a close. Hunting, drinking and socialising was their recreation, and life only became serious when local elections occurred and when parliament, with all its pomp and splendour, was called. The years flew quickly during the eighteenth century, with hardly a significant date noting a national alarm such as an uprising, battle or siege. All that changed, however, when 1798 dawned.

The
6 DAWN of
MODERN
TIMES

GALWAY'S LANDED GENTRY

AS **T**ʰᵉ **EIGHTEENTH CENTURY** drew to a close, County Galway boasted 'more gentlemen's seats than in any other part of Ireland'. Various records note over 400 landlords listed for the county in 1814, with families such as those associated with Clanricarde, Clonbrock, Dunsandle, Clancarty and Berridge owning a total of 300,000 acres (with Richard Berridge of Clifden Castle the lord of 160,152 acres) towards the end of the nineteenth century!

CLANRICARDE BURKES

Some of the largest proprietors of the best land in the east of the county were the Clanricarde Burkes whose estates were known as 'Clanricarde Country', consisting of 56,862 acres by 1883. Their main seat was at Portumna, where a stately 'castle' was erected overlooking the River Shannon by Richard Burke, 4th Earl of Clanricarde, about 1617. This large rectangular fortified mansion played its part in Galway's history, being the scene of the infamous Lord Strafford Commission in 1635. The building was accidentally burned down in 1826 and in recent times it has been re-roofed. It now contains a fine pictorial history of the old Clanricardes in all their aristocratic glory, finishing with Hubert, the 2nd Marquess and 15th Earl, who was such a formidable figure in the Land War.

Meanwhile, the fortunes of other branches of the family varied according to which side they took in several military actions of the seventeenth century, and some were well represented at gentry level with large estates and prominent houses as at Glinsk (of the MacDavid Burkes) and St Cleran's near Craughwell, later owned by John Huston, the famous American film director.

T*he* O'FLAHERTYS

Outside the Burke dynasty, the remaining Galway 'gentry' consisted mainly of four categories, the first of which were some old Irish clan families who were generally much reduced in wealth and influence in the aftermath of seventeenth-century wars and eighteenth-century Penal Laws. In the west the 'ferocious' O'Flahertys of Connemara paid the ultimate price for never conforming fully to English law.

Their once powerful base at Aughnanure Castle, near Oughterard, was captured by Sir Edward Fitton in 1572 and although re-granted to Hugh O'Flaherty in 1618, subsequent O'Flaherty involvement in the 1641 rebellion saw them dispossessed and their properties forfeited under the Cromwellian settlement Acts. The merchant Martins of Galway were transplanted or bought their way into most of these extensive western territories, while the principal western stronghold of the O'Flaherty clan at Bunowen Castle, south of Clifden, once home to Dónal 'an Chogaidh' (of the battle) and his illustrious wife, Grace O'Malley, was granted to the Geoghegans, a transplanted Catholic family from Westmeath.

Only the house and estate at Lemonfield beside Lough Corrib remained in O'Flaherty possession up to the 1930s, with J. P. O'Flaherty JP, a descendant of Murchadh 'na dTua' (of the battleaxe), the last resident. Most of the rest of the O'Flahertys were reduced to acting as simple caretakers on lands they once owned. This was the case with the present Renvyle House Hotel, which was part of the estate purchased by a branch of the Galway Blakes in 1680 from the Earl of Westmeath, who acquired it as forfeited land from the O'Flahertys. By the start of the nineteenth century the local O'Flahertys were simply acting as agents for the new owners, who dismissed them in 1810—a timid end to this branch of the once 'ferocious' clan.

OTHER NATIVE IRISH GENTRY

To the east of the county the descendants of other noted Irish clans also suffered greatly during these sad times of forfeiture and confiscations, including the Concannons, Mahons, McDermotts and Donellans. As well, the once proud O'Shaughnessys found their properties around Gort confiscated and acquired by the Prendergasts. Their neighbours, the O'Maddens, likewise saw part of their estates go to the Eyres, who built Eyrecourt mansion on these forfeited lands. The Seymours, who came as military officers, also acquired Madden land and, according to Patrick Melvin, a leading authority on Galway's landed gentry, built a residence on to the old Madden tower house at Ballymore.

The O'Kellys too, despite siding with local English forces against O'Sullivan Beare in 1603, saw their vast estates in the east of the county gradually whittle away as Cromwellian adventurers confiscated their properties. Thus the Blakeneys replaced the Kelly branch at Gallagh and named their new demesne Castleblakeney. Here also the newcomers added their new mansion to the older Kelly castle, a blend of old and new architectural styles also evident today at Tullira with the Martins, Castletaylor with the Taylors, and at Menlo with the Blakes. Meanwhile the Frenches took over Clogher from the Kellys and renamed the estate Castlefrench. The present Castle French House was built in 1779 by Sir Charles French and historical figures associated with it include Daniel O'Connell and President Éamon de Valera.

Perhaps the best-known act of this eighteenth-century version of ethnic cleansing involving the O'Kellys, had the Frenches move into their lands at Monivea, where the latter built Monivea Castle which, ironically, was eventually demolished by its last owner, the Irish state! On the death of Rosamond French in 1938, over 400 lots were auctioned including two Canaletto paintings which sold for £17 each! Today only the impressive French family mausoleum, a fine castellated structure in its own right, 'redolent of nineteenth-century craftsmanship' with its granite, marble and stained-glass interior, reminds us of the fickleness of wealth as the Frenches followed the Kellys into the setting sun of history.

1. **Athenry Castle**. Early type Norman castle built by Meiler de Bermingham in Athenry c. 1238. Originally two storeys in height, it was raised an extra floor in later years and is surrounded by a strong curtain wall. Now open to the public.

2. **Cleggan Court Tomb**. This Court Tomb at Cleggan is one of many prehistoric field monuments in this part of North-West Connemara. They indicate a comprehensive farming settlement there in Neolithic times.

(top right)
3. **Aerial photo of NUI, Galway**. Started in 1846 and completed in 1848, the construction of the new university building brought third-level education to Galway City, as well as giving much-needed employment to over 400 workers during the Great Famine.

(bottom right)
4. **Church of St Nicholas**. A rare view of the Church of St Nicholas in Galway in the interim period between the demolition of the Shambles Military Barracks and the construction of St Patrick's National School in 1954. It is Galway City's oldest building still in use.

5. **Clonfert Door**. Clonfert Cathedral contains the finest example of Hiberno/Romanesque doorway decoration in Ireland. An amazing array of carved motifs in stone display geometric designs as well as human and animal head forms to the highest degree of native craftsmanship.

6. **Derryhivenny Castle**. This is one of the last Tower Houses of over 270 built in County Galway between the 15th and 17th centuries. It was constructed in 1643 and still contains some of its original wood inserts.

7. **Dún Connor Stone Fort**. One of the great Celtic stone forts on the Aran Islands, this one on Inishmaan, vies with Dún Aengus on Inishmore for visitor attention. Debate still continues as to the actual purpose of these huge Iron Age stone structures.

8. **High Island**. The ruins of St Feicín's Early Christian monastic site rests beside the little lake, which supplied water as well as mill power to 7th-century monks on this high-rise Atlantic island off the coast of Clifden. As the photo shows, the ancient buildings, church and cells are being conserved.

(top right)
9. **Kilmacduagh Monastic Site**. Kilmacduagh is one of Ireland's most famous Early Christian monastic sites, founded by St Colman Mac Duagh in the 7th century. It contains a number of later church ruins including a cathedral, as well as a Round Tower which leans nearly a metre from the perpendicular, reminding one of its counterpart in Pisa.

(bottom right)
10. **Kilbannon Round Tower outside Tuam**. Founded by St Benin, a disciple of St Patrick, this partially ruined Round Tower, one of six in County Galway, is part of the collection of Christian monuments, which makes Tuam the ecclesiastical heart of County Galway.

11. **Loughrea Cathedral**. Loughrea Cathedral, dating from the start of the 20th century, was the catalyst which led to the Celtic Revival of Irish craftsmanship in stained glass, stone sculpture, as well as iron and woodworking of the highest order. Beside it is pictured the memorial to Fr Michael Griffin, murdered during the 'Troubles' in Galway City.

12. **Thoor Ballylee**. Once owned by the Burkes, this, the most famous of all Galway's Tower Houses, was restored by W. B. Yeats 'for his wife, George'; they lived there during the 1920s. It is now a heritage centre dedicated to this great poet, complete with display facilities explaining the unique literary heritage attached to the castle and district.

13. Portumna Castle. This fine early 17th-century castellated mansion dating from c.1617 became th main seat of the Clanricarde Burkes until it was destroyed by fire in 1826. Much restoration work ha seen it reopen in recent times as a heritage centre devoted to the history of the Clanricardes.

14. Turoe Stone. The wonder of curvilinear La Tène Celtic art is displayed in its full splendour on th carved erratic at Turoe, just north of Loughrea. Many other examples of similarly inscribed stones a to be seen in Brittany in France, indicating the movement pattern of the Celts in the centuries befo Christ.

5. Tyrone House. This fine example of the Teach Mór or landlord's 'Big House' near Clarinbridge once belonged to the St George family and clearly shows the fate which befell so many of these impressive 18/19th-century mansions when it was torched by local Irish Volunteers during the Fight for Independence.

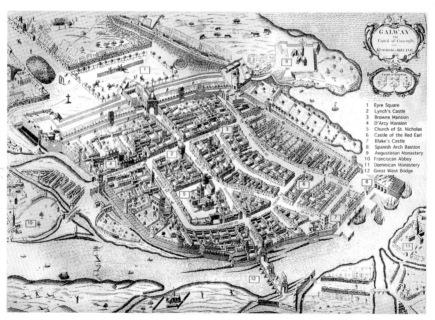

16. Pictorial Map of Galway. Commissioned, it seems, before the Cromwellian/ Parliamentarian siege of Galway 1651–2, this map, Galway's most treasured artefact, was probably completed during the reign of Charles II to illustrate the town's loyalty to the Crown. The street patterns depicted are unaltered today.

17. **Lynch's Castle**. Lynch's Castle in Shop Street, Galway, shortly after it was enlarged, is depicted in this illustration from Hall's *Ireland, its Scenery, Character*, published in 1842. The Lynchs were Galway's leading merchants, providing 84 mayors to the town before the Parliamentarian siege of 1651–2. Hood-mouldings over windows give a medieval ambience to the scene.

18. **Robert O'Hara Burke, Explorer of Australia**. Francis Chamberlain (*front, centre*), grandson of former British Prime Minister, Neville Chamberlain, and descendant of Robert O'Hara Burke, stares intently at a Galway Civic Trust plaque he has just unveiled in Dominick Street, Galway, in memory of the great Galway-born Australian explorer.
(© *Connacht Tribune*)

19. **County Galway Courthouse and Jail.** This 1820 illustration from James Hardiman's *History of Galway* depicts the County Courthouse erected in 1815, newly connected by the Salmon Weir Bridge (1819) with the County and City jails (1802–10) so that convicted felons could start their sentences immediately! Starving people sought 'refuge' in this jail during the Great Famine!

20. **Pádraic Ó Conaire.** Ó Conaire was County Galway's famous writer in Gaelic, who pioneered the Irish literary revival in the native tongue. Author of many books and articles, a columnist with the *Connacht Sentinel* newspaper, and a teacher, Pádraic died in 1928. His statue by Albert Power graced Eyre Square until its removal to the city museum.

21. **Pope John Paul II in Ballybrit.** The greatest gathering on Galway soil took place at Ballybrit Racecourse on 30 September 1979 when the Pope paid his historic visit to Galway, prior to flying on to Knock. It was here that he took the 'young people of Ireland' to his heart. (Courtesy Galway Diocesan Archives)

22. **President Kennedy in Galway.** Great excitement is evident in the faces of the animated spectators as President John F. Kennedy makes his way to Eyre Square in June 1963, where he gave an inspiring speech to massed thousands, just a few months before he was assassinated in Dallas. (© *Connacht Tribune*)

23. **Corrib Estuary, 1820.** This engraving from James Hardiman's *History of Galway* shows Galway City from the Claddagh shoreline. Galway hookers gather around the former medieval harbour downstream from the Great West Bridge, while ocean-going craft are berthed in the Mud Dock at the end of Eyre's Long Walk.

24. **Claddagh Village, 1928.** This aerial photograph of the old Claddagh fishing village or clachan shows the 'Big Grass' area in the bottom left section, with Fairhill Road leading away to the left, in 1928, the same year that the village was condemned under the Health Acts of the day. The village was subsequently demolished.

25. **Claregalway Abbey, Castle and Bridge**. Much detail is evident in this 1842 engraving for Hall's *Ireland, its Scenery, Character*. The Franciscan Abbey is outlined against the evening sun, as is the much-ivied and ruined Clanricarde Castle, while a coach hurries homeward over the Bridge of Nine Arches, now recently restored.

26. **Lynch Memorial Window**. The world's first official tourist trap, the Lynch Memorial Window in Market Street, Galway, commemorates the public hanging (lynching?) by the Mayor of Galway of his own son in 1493 over 'an affair of the heart', supposedly from the displayed window, a deed which never really happened.

GALWAY TRIBES AS LANDED GENTRY

The descendants of the merchant princes of Galway town who had acquired vast estates throughout Connacht in the seventeenth century from legal dealings were the second category of landlords of which the Frenches, with their main seats at Monivea and Castlefrench, were prime examples.

The Blakes were much noted also on the Galway gentry landscape with over 30 houses to their credit including those at Menlo, Furbo, Ardfry, Corbally, Ballyglunin and the aforementioned Renvyle House, to mention just a few. Today their partially restored town mansion known as K.C. Blake's Brasserie Restaurant is only one of two town castles existing in Galway City.

Meanwhile, only a fine doorway of the Darcy mansion stands today in the grounds of the Mercy Convent to remind us of the Darcy presence in Galway town, but this once powerful merchant family also left its mark in the landed properties of the county as well. Estates at Kiltullagh and Newforest, as well as the town of Clifden, founded by John Darcy in the early years of the nineteenth century, indicate the family's important position among the landed gentry of the time.

MARTYNS/MARTINS

While the Lynchs were also former large landowners in the county, it is the Martins or Martyns who attracted most attention. As mentioned earlier, the Martins gained most of Connemara from the O'Flahertys in the wake of Cromwellian settlements, and in spite of fighting on the Jacobite side at the Battle of Aughrim, 'Nimble' Dick Martin was able to hold on to his Connemara estate of nearly a quarter of a million acres by, it seems, his 'nimble' use of words of regret.

Building great houses at Birchall, Ross, and Dangan beside Lough Corrib, their main residence became Ballinahinch Castle in South Connemara, which started as an inn in 1819 but was remodelled in the 'castle' mould by the most famous of the family, Richard (Humanity Dick) Martin MP, who was instrumental in founding the Society for the Prevention of Cruelty to Animals in England. Known also as 'Hair-Trigger Dick' for his duelling prowess, he ruled Connemara like a feudal prince from Ballinahinch, boasted of having the longest driveway in the land (some 25 miles to Oughterard), and that the King's writ stopped at the entrance to that driveway!

Meanwhile east of Galway town, another branch of the Martin family, with their surname changed to Martyn, retained Tullira Castle and estate near Gort while still remaining Catholic by way of royal privilege for aiding Protestants during difficult times.

TRANSPLANTED GENTRY

Another category of the landed gentry were those Catholic families transplanted into Galway during the 'Hell or to Connacht' plantation times of the seventeenth century. As mentioned earlier, the Geoghegans arrived in Connemara from Westmeath, while the Bellews came from Louth, the Cheevers from Meath and the Nugents to Pallas from Westmeath.

PROTESTANT LANDLORDS

The fourth and most influential category of landlords were those of the Protestant faith, which some native Catholic families adopted fully or nominally in order to hold on to land. Others were introduced to the Galway countryside because of their Protestant birth mainly as a result of the Cromwellian or Williamite invasions. Of the former the Clanricardes led the way, of course, but others who conformed to the Established Church included, according to Melvin, the Dalys of Dunsandle, the Kellys of Castle Kelly, the Dillons of Clonbrock and the Prendergasts of Lough Cutra as well as the aforementioned Martins.

Meanwhile, the more important Protestant families who acquired land in the wake of seventeenth-century confiscations included the Eyres, the Trenches, the Gregorys and the Persses, while the Wades and Seymours were also newcomers to the county scene. The Eyres, who also acquired property on the periphery of Galway town, including Eyre Square, and who added Long Walk and its mud dock to the town topography, also created important estates on former Madden lands at Eyrecourt and Eyreville.

The Trenches, however, were the most important of these newcomers, settling mostly in Garbally at Ballinasloe and Woodlawn. Marrying into the transplanted Power family from Cork, they acquired more land in this eastern section of the county, often buying forfeited properties formerly owned by the merchant tribes of Galway.

The Persse family got large land grants also, displacing, for instance, the Burkes of Isertkelly and eventually the Burkes of Moyode. With them came members of the Gregory family who acquired the Kinvara estate as well as the Coole and Kiltartan estates from wealth accumulated in India. As can be expected, there was much intermarriage among these upper classes, perhaps the most famous that between Isabella (Augusta) Persse (better known as Lady Gregory) of Roxborough and Sir William Gregory of Coole Park later in the nineteenth century, which had such a profound effect on the literary life of Ireland.

LATE 18TH-CENTURY POLITICS

As the eighteenth century drew to its close, politics, not literature, occupied the minds of the gentry then, leading at times to confrontations at polling booths, courthouses and in the two parliaments of the time. Although in parliamentary elections in town and county Protestant political control was complete, the real question facing the voter was whether to support the more conservative Whigs or to vote for the Tories, who favoured a less repressive attitude towards Catholicism.

Complicating matters even more were the influences exerted on the ruling classes from the political fall-out of the French and American Revolutions towards the end of the century. More alarming still was the possibility of hostilities breaking out between France and England and the subsequent threat of invasion, especially through the open port of Galway.

GALWAY VOLUNTEERS

The consequential loss of property and privilege concentrated minds and with no militia raised by the government to offset troop depletion caused by the American campaigns, a new local force called the Irish Volunteers was formed. Raised by landed gentry and the professional classes in the cities to face any invasion threat, the new corps leaders also saw the need of the right to independence of the Irish Parliament, and in reflecting the changing times, a relaxation of the Penal Laws. With Henry Grattan to the fore on the political stage, the Act of Repeal was announced on 21 June 1782, leading to much rejoicing especially in the towns and villages of County Galway.

This was only to be expected, because as early as 1777 the first unit of the Volunteers in Connacht was formed by Colonel William Persse on his Roxborough estate. Named as the Roxborough Volunteers, they were soon joined by local groups enjoying such jingoistic titles as the Clanricarde Cavalry, Chasseurs and Infantry under the Earl of Clanricarde, the Headford Volunteers under Col Redington, the Galway Chasseurs under Col St George French, the Galway Artillery and Independents under Col Martin, the Gort Light Dragoons, the Tuam Volunteers, the Loughrea Artillery, the Eyrecourt Buffs, and even the Derrymacloghny Volunteers.

These were heady days indeed in Galway as the spirit of nationalism, albeit based mostly on a Protestant power base, permeated the countryside. However, change was coming too quickly for the Establishment, and the fear of granting the right to arms and legislature to Catholics was too much for many of the delegates at the various national conventions of the Volunteers, and consequently the movement went into terminal decline.

NEW MILITARY FORMATIONS

The beginning of the end came in 1793 with the passing of the Militia Act, which saw a more reliable local military force under the Earl of Clancarty being raised with its HQ at Garbally outside Ballinasloe. That same year also saw the formation of the Connaught Rangers under royal commission by John Thomas de Burgh, brother of Henry, 12th Earl of Clanricarde, while the raising of a yeomanry force in 1796 finally rang the death knell for the former Volunteer corps. Meanwhile, any hope of a French or American-style revolution entertained by Irish Catholics disappeared with the Act of Union of 1800, which underlined the total authority of the English Parliament over the two islands.

Yet things were improving on the Catholic front in Galway town as the eighteenth century drew to a close. With less than 400 Protestants out of a population of over 14,000 in the 1760s, attention was now turned to economic matters rather than religious dominance, as evidenced by the relaxation of the Penal Laws in various Acts during the years 1778 and 1782, which saw the right to lease or own property, and the setting up of educational institutions, returned to the majority. Freedom to profess one's religion was still restricted, however, and while the move for Catholic emancipation was slowly gaining ground, the citizens of Galway remained loyal to the Crown. That loyalty was to be tested when the French landed in Killala in 1798.

FIGHTING The FRENCH

While the noble ideals of liberty, equality and fraternity were gaining strength in Ireland at the close of the eighteenth century, the reality on the ground in Galway town was continued loyalty to the English throne at a time when economic prosperity was returning through industrial expansion and religious restrictions, especially at local level, were more honoured in the breach than in the observance.

Thus General Humbert and his French expeditionary force were seen by the town authorities as a danger to the status quo and had to be opposed. Within half an hour of word of the landing, the town merchants collected the quite large sum of 1,500 guineas to enable the town garrison, as well as the local yeoman cavalry, to march northwards and stop the French in their tracks. Unfortunately, these forces didn't exactly cover themselves in glory when they participated in the general rout known as 'The Races of Castlebar', at which Humbert and his gathering band of Mayo supporters won their only major military engagement. This victory was short-lived, however, and when the invasion collapsed at Ballinamuck some days later, retribution on the Irish contingent was harsh in the extreme.

While individual Galway supporters of the invasion were also singled out for punishment, and Claregalway Friary chapel was damaged by demoralised government troops retreating from Castlebar, the fact remains that in their absence Catholic clergy, led by an Augustinian friar guarding the Great West Bridge, ensured that peace prevailed in the town of Galway. This loyalty did not go unnoticed among the ruling Protestant minority, who thereafter came to the fore in advocating Catholic emancipation as a result.

INCREASED DEFENCES

Just as pressing for both sides of the religious divide, however, was the need to increase economic prosperity at county as well as Galway town level once the invasion threat from France was averted following the collapse of the Killala adventure, and the need to upgrade both river and maritime defences

Examples of the former occurred at the vulnerable bridge over the Shannon at Banagher where the Fanesker fort was erected c. 1812, while new maritime defences consisted of Martello Towers being constructed at Finavarra Point and Aughinish on the southern shores of Galway Bay and another at Rossaveal in Connemara.

CHANGING ECONOMIC CONDITIONS

As the nineteenth century dawned, times were certainly changing in Galway town and county. From near economic stagnation as a result of the restrictive Penal Laws, when only freemen of the town could employ themselves in mercantile affairs at the start of the eighteenth century, Galway town finally found new life towards the end of that century when entrepreneurs came to add new and exciting industrial skills to those of the trading kind practised by the descendants of the original merchant tribes. It had taken a long time, the whole of the eighteenth century in fact, to lay the modern economic foundations of the town.

By then the beef export trade in particular had gone into decline as the cold wind of economic reality sent an extra chill along these old worn quays. Connacht cattle were now being driven into the rich grazing lands of Munster by the new, emerging landed gentry, most of whom had little affinity with the ancient town of Galway. Higher prices filled their silk-lined pockets as they sent their expanding herds southwards via the famous October fair at Ballinasloe. Consequently, ports such as Cork, Limerick and Waterford began to profit at Galway's expense.

DECLINING PORT

Worse was to follow for the declining western port. A growing population, even one as poor as that in the town and surrounding countryside, welcomed the increasing numbers and variety of household goods coming to market from mainland Britain. Instead of being imported through Galway port, however, the bulk of such items were carried overland along the emerging roadway networks by dealers operating from a booming Dublin port.

Not surprisingly, Galway's mercantile prosperity was in serious decline when only 20 sailing vessels docked annually by 1760 and international trade had reached its lowest ebb as the eighteenth century entered its last quarter. Another problem facing Galway's merchants was the dangerous condition of the town quays and piers situated upstream of the Spanish Arch bastion.

Galway Corporation was much maligned for allowing its harbour infrastructure to fall into a state rendering it unsafe to load or unload vessels over 30 tons. At a time when shipping tonnage was increasing, it was obvious that a new harbour facility had to be provided as Galway slipped to only eighth position in the list of Irish ports. It came from an unexpected source.

EYRE'S LONG WALK *and* DOCK

Previously, a wall walk directly downstream of the Spanish Arch bastion leading to a new salmon netting station, called the Crow's Rock, had been completed in 1643. Eventually, direct access to the walkway and an emerging wasteland from river silting was provided by the insertion in the old city wall extension of what is today called the Spanish Arch.

This arch allowed, in time, the walkway to be enlarged by Edward Eyre by 1739, as well as the building of a row of houses along what was to become known as Eyre's Long Walk, at the end of which a new dry dock, the disused Mud Dock of today, was also constructed. Private initiative rather than municipal effort had saved the day.

Soon, fresh activities were noted at Eyre's dock where imports consisted of iron, steel, coal and timber from Scandinavia and America, while some wine still came from Spain. Meanwhile, shipments of flax seed from America, started by Andrew French in 1760, helped revive the ailing local linen industry.

Evidence of this revival was later noted on the quayside when the *Connaught Journal* of 28 November 1791 reported:

> *Last Saturday the ship* Minerva, *burthen about 400 tons, the property of Messrs. Walter and John Burke, was launched from the building yard on the Quay amidst several thousand spectators, who arrived from different parts of the country, to enjoy the pleasing sight of the largest ship that has ever been constructed here. The vessel was launched with facility and safety, which added to the satisfaction of the spectators. Many families during this scarce season were maintained by the employment, which the construction of the* Minerva *procured for them.*

Within a few short years many families were being maintained by new employment as the town's waterways powered Galway into the Industrial Revolution during the first half of the nineteenth century. Meanwhile, their country cousins were also benefiting from changing economic and political circumstances.

LAND TENURE

Ever-increasing numbers of displaced tenants were settling in the western counties after grazing substituted much intensive farming in the east with the ending of the Napoleonic Wars in 1815, while tenant populations increased naturally from using the new potato crops as an invaluable food source. Life was, in the main, harsh, especially for those forced to operate the clachan/rundale system in the rough lands of the western seaboard.

Here, groups of displaced families collectively rented land from the local landlord, and having built their little thatched homes adjacent to one another in clachans or small villages, they shared the precious arable land for tillage purposes while using the rough upper lands as commonage for grazing their small stock herds during the summer months.

In this situation the potato-filled 'lazy beds' provided the main food source, while other crops and meagre profits from animal husbandry helped pay the rent and provided a little extra for the simple luxuries of their harsh lifestyles.

While the landlord agents lived in larger houses and enjoyed a higher standard of living, the main beneficiaries of the system were of course the landed gentry. While some became absentee landlords, living off the proceeds of their tenants' rent, others spent lives of luxury on their vast estates hunting with the County Galway Hunt, which was formed in the County Courthouse in 1839. Some, however, sought to improve their farm production schemes, and even in some instances the lot of their tenants.

LAND PRODUCTION

The main production lines of these landlord estates were of wool and beef on the hoof, which increased greatly with the relaxation of export restriction laws for cattle in 1758, for sheep in 1759, and for beef in 1776. Due to these restrictions sheep products could not really compete with the English mainland providers and the main marketing of mutton and wool was for the home market centred mainly in Dublin. Some of the important producers of sheep in Galway were the Trenches of Woodlawn, the Bellews of Mountbellew and the Frenches of Monivea, with the Ballinasloe Fair the central market for wool, at which both landlord and tenant sold fleeces.

Cattle-raising was the main component of the livestock industry in County Galway, however, and with free trade coming into play at the end of the eighteenth century, as well as provisions needed in Britain during its war with France, exports of cattle on the hoof and beef to Britain increased. Both grazing and the fattening of cattle was carried out on the vast estates of the eastern section of the county, with some landlords renting parts of their lands to large-scale graziers.

Many of these graziers farmed part of their rented lands, thus laying the foundation of the later 'large farmer' class, who in turn rented up to 100 acres to 'smaller farmers'. At the bottom of the scale were the cottiers living in simple cabins with a half-acre or so of land devoted to potatoes, which they paid for in cash or labour.

Many of the same landed gentry engaged in large-scale cattle-raising, with Ballinasloe and Dunmore hosting the main fairs, as did Fair Hill in the Claddagh area of Galway town, arising from a patent granted to Nicholas Darcy in 1613. By 1820 another fair held at Eyre Square on 31 May 'principally for black cattle' was becoming more popular. By tradition as well as law, however, the event at Fair Hill was the important one for cattle, sheep and horses.

Sadly, in 1828 up to 20 people from Annaghdown were drowned in a River Corrib disaster, with the sinking of a sailing craft ferrying them to that same fair at Fair Hill. Not long afterwards the famous bard, Anthony Raftery, wrote his epic poem, 'Anach Chuain', commemorating this tragic event.

With increasing demands for farm produce such as beef, wool and wheat, as the Napoleonic Wars intensified at the start of the nineteenth century, County Galway land users, from landlord to small farmer, did their utmost to satisfy the demands from 'across the water'. While some cereal production was left mostly to producers in the east of the country, Galway's 'improving' landlords also sought to install mini industries on their estates. An example of this was the linen industry, which had increased by the 1750s after the Linen Board was founded in 1711.

The French family of Monivea was one of the main promoters of the linen trade, setting up a bleach mill and green in the new village of Monivea, with eight weavers being brought in to start the trade. In 1776 there were 276 weavers' houses as well as 370 wheels on the estate. By 1817, however, the recession following the Napoleonic Wars, augmented by the arrival of power-spinning in Ulster, led to the general decline of the industry in County Galway. Only the wide green lawns of Monivea village today recall the time when home crafts and industry played an important role in the economic life of Galway families. In the town of Galway, though, things were improving for its citizens as the economic stagnation of the eighteenth century finally came to an end.

EARLY GALWAY INDUSTRIES

In full flow the River Corrib is a massive sight of natural power as 10,000 cubic feet of water per second is discharged over the Salmon

Weir barrage in the heart of Galway town. At the start of the nineteenth century during the Industrial Revolution in Britain, this massive display of nature's power drew special attention. Not surprisingly, a whole new class of entrepreneurs emerged which saw the potential of industrial development inherent in the town's waterways.

Within a few short years the leading position of the merchant trader gave way to the industrialist, who turned around the town's ailing economy, transformed its waterways into centres of industrial might, and created family fortunes for the Ireland, Reagan and Murray families in particular.

This is clearly evident in the flour-milling industry, which had long progressed beyond the Clybaun horizontal mill dating to about AD 600, once harnessing the little stream flowing through the heart of the western suburb of Galway City today. From Norman times milling families had made their living, as well as their fortunes, on the superior powers of the vertical mill wheel. From 1558 when Thomas Martin was granted a patent to build a flour mill on the western banks of the River Corrib, to countless other mills dotting town, village or countryside, the groan of the water wheel had become the sound of industrial might.

Thus, flour milling has a long history in County Galway, especially in the area nurtured by the warm limestone soils stretching from Kinvara to Gort. Here as the nineteenth century dawned, wheat became an even more viable raw material and, just as important, was only a day's cart journey from the new and numerous grindstones awaiting business all along the banks of the River Corrib.

While just two flour mills operated in Galway town in 1790, the number expanded to 23 by 1820, augmented by six oat mills, all of which were making good use of 'the fall and rapidity of the river'. Soon upwards of 12,000 tons of wheat were being processed annually by the various mills, causing over 20 tall, ancillary flour and grain stores to rise over the newly formed and appropriately named Merchants Road as well as the new, fashionable houses verging Eyre Square.

GALWAY TOWN EXPANSIONS

As the nineteenth century progressed, the town of Galway was prosperous again with industry providing the basis of unprecedented economic growth, which in turn led to an explosion in the population figures as workers flooded in from outlying areas seeking employment. Hardiman, writing his famous *History of Galway* in 1820, suggested that the real population figure for Galway town was over 40,000 as against the figure of 24,711 recorded by the first census carried out in 1812.

Housing such a rising number of people was a big problem, with the majority living in terrible squalor in the centre of the city. Home now to many families were the crumbling mansions of the former medieval merchants. The refurbishment of these old buildings consisted simply of plastering the façades and, in some cases, even lowering and repairing the roofs of the more derelict examples.

On the western outskirts, new streets were being added in the Nuns Island, Henry Street and Dominick Street areas, with the latter housing the new managerial classes in expressive, three-storey cut stone buildings. One became the town house of the O'Hara Burkes, whose country estate was at St Cleran's near Craughwell. James Hardiman Burke was elected mayor in 1820 and his son Robert O'Hara Burke became the famous explorer of Australia who pioneered the first south/north crossing of that great continent in 1860–1, unfortunately losing his life in the attempt.

T𝒽e CLADDAGH

Meanwhile on the western shore of the River Corrib estuary, the ancient Gaelic Claddagh fishing village was expanding also, due to supplying fish to the town on a commercial basis after the demise of the Blakes, the town's fish merchants for generations. Operating from Galway hookers, their famous black-hulled and brown-sailed fishing craft, the Claddonians increased their annual sea harvest by the start of the nineteenth century, and wealth flowed into the village.

With more of the young villagers marrying girls from Aran and the Connemara coastline, the number of thatched homes increased in the Claddagh to 468, and the population to 3,000 by 1820. Although the fishing industry with all its rules and regulations was controlled by an annually elected king, the village was effectively ruled by the women, who sold the catch from the family boat and banked the household revenue in the safety of the deep pockets of their práiscín aprons.

As a result, the village expanded about the Dominican Church, known as St Mary's on the Hill. The main portion of the village spread westwards from the Big Grass area along the winding road of Fair Hill, and eastwards around the Garra Glas area, where the Galway fire station is located today.

Overall, this expansion in the entire urban area, as well as growth in population, industry and commerce in the early years of the nineteenth century was based on improving national as well as local government infrastructures. Both had been evolving in Galway for a long time.

RULE Of LAW

When the county system was established in the late sixteenth century, the Lord Deputy's first duty was to elect the county sheriff, who acted as the chief administrator in each county. It was his brief to ensure the proper administration of civil and criminal affairs in the county, select the County Grand Jury (the major organ of local administration until the advent of the County Councils in 1898/9), and to act as returning officer for the various parliamentary elections which saw each county as well as eight urban ones (including Galway town) return two members of parliament.

Law was administered when the King's judges visited each county twice yearly (spring and summer) during the assizes, and they were assisted by grand juries, usually made up of 23 members from the more important local gentry stock or town dignitaries.

An important function of assizes sessions was the involvement of the visiting magistrate in the widely used 'Presentment' proceedings. The treasurer of the Grand Jury organised the cess or tax to finance the contract, which was to be collected from the propertied gentlemen of the district, and after verification of the proper completion of the work he paid the parties involved. Through this method hundreds of rural and public urban schemes were carried out, ranging from ten bridges built in the county in 1795 (including the four-arched example at Oranmore) to the famous 'Beggers' Bridge' constructed in 1826–7 at a cost of £366. 5. 0 next to the main entrance of Galway City's Cathedral on University Road.

Meanwhile, the most important local courts consisted of the Quarter Sessions which were presided over by Protestant landlords, often with little training or experience. Subsequent to 1827, however, after much-needed revision, Petty Sessions involving two or more judges were held twice a year in Loughrea, Tuam, Eyrecourt and Gort.

After 1836 newly appointed resident magistrates, made famous by the *Irish R.M.* television series (based partly on the writings of Violet Martin of Ross, Moycullen), reported monthly to the chief secretary on their districts, as unrest particularly from food shortages began to be reported. In the various boroughs set up under Norman times Borough Courts were held, as in Tuam, with the head of the local corporation presiding.

Interestingly, while the county courthouse and jail was situated in Galway town, the city also had its own jail and courthouse, the latter eventually becoming the Town Hall Theatre. To back up the law, there were also bridewells (temporary lock-up facilities) in Ballinasloe, Gort, Loughrea, Tuam, Woodford, Eyrecourt and Clifden.

GUARDIANS Of The PEACE

With a population expanding, perhaps too rapidly for the political and social conditions pertaining at the time, these various courts were becoming much frequented as the nineteenth century progressed. With local food shortages being reported in 1816–17, 1831 and especially in 1842, resulting in food riots in Galway town, security at local as well as national level was all important as the century progressed. In town and county, both the military and a growing constabulary presence ensured that insurrection as seen in Mayo and Wexford in the closing decade of the eighteenth century would not happen in Galway.

A start had been made in the aftermath of the seventeenth-century sieges, when Galway became even more a 'garrison town' with a Lower Citadel built to guard the West Bridge and an Upper Citadel constructed near the main city gate facing Eyre Square, now the site of the Edward Square Shopping Mall. In 1749 the Lower Citadel was converted into the Shambles Barracks and garrisoned with ten companies, which by 1837 consisted of 15 officers and 326 other ranks. Earlier, in 1734 the Upper Citadel was provided with 'a proper barracks for three companies', and by 1837 its troop complement consisted of six officers and 130 other ranks as well as a hospital for 60 patients.

Across County Galway military barracks were established in Loughrea, Gort, Dunmore, Ballinasloe and Oughterard, while there were also 99 constabulary stations with over 600 constables and sub-constables to police the county.

EARLY ROADS

With security tightened, communication networks especially by road found early prioritisation. While a Road Act was passed in 1613 which made each parish responsible for the maintenance of its roads, a more popular system was the Presentment model operated by the Grand Jury which commenced in 1634 and lasted right down to 1899, when the County Councils were inaugurated. This system allowed for 13 or more jurors (usually landlords or their agents) to present payments within a county for public works done (such as road-building), with revenue for such schemes to be levied as a tax on land.

Thus, the first roadways came into being with major transport routes initially radiating out from Dublin as presented on some of the early single-line strip road maps, such as the famous Taylor and Skinner maps of 1778, which simply displayed lines linking the main towns. While these showed the distances between Dublin and Galway via Loughrea as marked by eighteenth-century milestones, earlier stones suggest that the initial main west/east roadway ran through Ahascragh and Menlough to Galway. In the western section of the county, only a rough roadway ran as far as Oughterard, with perhaps the Martins supplying one of the two surviving milestones on that route.

At this time also the need for improved surveying techniques arose in the case of estate and county maps such as that by William Larkin in 1819, which helped in the computation of County Galway's cess or tax. Later on, Scottish engineer Alexander Nimmo helped commence roadways, eventually reaching as far as Clifden as well as to the little sea fishing village around his pier at Roundstone. His work would later help in opening up Connemara for the famous Bianconi coach transport company, whose Galway town depot was situated behind the Imperial Hotel of today.

Also coming into the picture at this time was an improving postal service which, with the establishment of the 'Connacht Road' in 1659, saw the first embryonic mail service starting in Galway. While mail coaches were introduced to Ireland in 1789, we have to wait until 1807 for an improved public coach transport scheme between Galway and Dublin. As mail charges were paid by the mile, it was imperative to improve the major road system in the county and to mark distances with milestones.

As Connemara was benefiting from its first true roadway leading to the newly founded town of Clifden in the early decades of the nineteenth century, many secondary ones were established as a result of the Presentment system and were starting to vein the eastern sections of the county also. On occasions local landlords were very much involved. For instances, the rather expressive milestone at Annagh Cross on the Galway/Roscommon Road carries the name of John Bodkin, Esq.

Transport by water, especially by sea, was also increasing as the nineteenth century progressed and it soon became obvious that a new harbour was needed for the expanding town of Galway. With increased industrial output the eighteenth-century Mud Dock was already becoming obsolete, while easy access between the sea and Lough Corrib was also an imperative as well as linking Ballinasloe to the Shannon via the River Suck.

NEW JAILS

In the meantime, major building schemes, giving welcome employment, were taking place in the town itself. With increasing levels of crime becoming evident from a burgeoning population, the start of the nineteenth century saw a huge jail complex being constructed on the west bank of the River Corrib at Nuns Island. Initially intended to be the county jail, which would replace the current one in the old Blake's Castle at the end of Quay Street, removed there from Loughrea in 1674, both town and county combined to establish this new jail in 1810. The original Town Jail was in Mainguard Street where, as usual for the time, more attention was paid to the security of the inmates than to their health or convenience.

The new jail was something else, however, with the city section three storeys in height as compared to two for the larger, crescent-shaped county section designed to hold 110 prisoners, all surrounded by a massive wall 20 ft high. The site of the jails was judiciously chosen with 'good air and excellent water' being noted, with two pounds of bread distributed daily to prisoners. However the harshness of the prison regime was indicated by the fact that no wood was used in the building, with iron and stone being in every instance substituted. An interesting comparison with jails today is that both institutions contained plenty of space for debtors!

With new jails, however, one needed courthouses to serve them, and between 1812 and 1815 the current county courthouse was erected on the site of the former Franciscan Abbey. Facing it across Courthouse Square, the town courthouse was completed in 1824, before town and county amalgamated to use the county version, while in time the town courthouse became the Town Hall Theatre of today.

GALWAY HARBOUR DEVELOPMENT

Other areas of employment in the early years of the nineteenth century saw the need for harbour and fishery development all along the Galway sea coast. By 1822 the aforementioned Scottish engineer, Alexander Nimmo, was busy building piers, and a breakwater to facilitate the Claddagh fishing fleet at low water at the mouth of the Corrib River bears his name today. Other Galway harbour improvements were to follow in the vicinity of the Claddagh Church, with the newly appointed Commissioners of Fisheries building quays and piers for the booming Claddagh fishery.

The main concern, however, was the need for a deep-water harbour as the Mud Dock facility became increasingly incapable of servicing the growing industrial sector. By the 1820s there was a need to construct a commercial dock to service in particular the vast array of stores and buildings already lining the new Merchants Road, which now fringed the vast, open salt marsh to the south.

The welcome establishment of the Galway Harbour Commissioners by way of a Parliamentary Act of 1830, incorporating initially some 63 commissioners, saw work commence in 1833 on what is today the Commercial Dock, a large (for its time) L-shaped floating dock of nearly seven acres in extent. The work was finally completed at a cost of £40,000 in 1842, which gave Galway one of the finest harbour facilities in the country.

BOARD of WORKS

Perhaps the most important state body founded in the early decades of the nineteenth century, which was to have such an enormous effect on local infrastructure, was the Board of Works, which in reality was a con-solidation of agencies dealing with government grants and loans, and with authority to finance public works or appropriate projects by suit-able bodies. Commencing in 1831, it was soon involved in an increasing number of projects such as maintaining public relief roads constructed during a mini famine in 1822, as well as constructing canals, bridges, waterway drainage, fishery piers, and public buildings ranging from post offices to police barracks and schools.

Practically every district in County Galway benefited from work carried out by this important agency, and none were so welcome from an employment point of view than in the dreadful days of the Great Famine. A hint of what was to come manifested itself with smaller famines in 1822 and 1831, followed by food riots in Galway town in 1842.

ABOLITION of TOWN CORPORATIONS

By 1835, with over two million people without regular employment in Ireland due to the flooding of the British market with cheaper and better products from the Continent, it was becoming obvious that local administration and health care procedures were becoming completely inadequate as destitution spread through town and county, especially in the western sections of the country.

In fact, local administration was in complete disarray in Galway town where, under continuous Daly family mayoralships, Galway Corporation had neglected its essential services. Consequently, as a result of the Corporations Act of 1840, the Corporations of Galway, Tuam and Athenry were abolished and replaced by Town Commissioners.

LOCAL HEALTH CARE

Meanwhile, the primitive health care procedures of the time were coming under ever-increasing pressure. At the start of the nineteenth century upwards of 20,000 people crowded the centre of Galway town, living mostly in unsanitary conditions leading to child mortality, disease and sickness. Increased state involvement was already evident in the presence of new courthouses and jails as well as a new custom house constructed in Flood Street. As the century commenced, the state finally looked to the health of the people in a more meaningful manner.

Previously, a seventeenth-century infirmary at Woodquay had been replaced by another of 'superior accommodation' in Abbeygate Street which, according to an eighteenth-century report, was an old house with two rooms on two floors. Obviously, something had to be done, and by 1802 a new County Infirmary, a 'spacious and elegant building' over-looking both bay and river, came to grace the heights of Prospect Hill on the main road into Galway town. While it was expected to treat up to 800 county patients annually, it was not until 1842 that the infirmary of the new workhouse catered for patients from the actual borough area.

Medical care increased greatly with the opening of the Galway Fever Hospital on Earl's Island, a building which is now incorporated into the NUI, Galway Centre for Human Rights complex. From 40–60 patients could be treated and it was put into immediate use during an outbreak of typhus in 1822 in the town, as well as catering for patients from Oughterard, Loughrea, Ardrahan and Kilcolgan, while an outbreak in North Galway had treatment provided at Ballygaddy House in Tuam, which was used as a temporary fever hospital. All the outbreaks were the result of a major failure of the potato crop which saw many starving farming families flock into Galway from Connemara, again an omen of what was to come.

Other relief agencies operating at the start of the century included a Connacht District Lunatic Asylum, which opened in Ballinasloe in 1833, and the Mendicity Institute off Francis Street, established in 1824 for 'miserable mendicants and vagrants' in Galway town.

RELIGIOUS ORDERS ARRIVE

A major boost to welfare came from the valiant efforts of newly arriving Religious Orders such as the Presentation Nuns who, as well as opening a school in the former Protestant Charter School premises in 1814, also provided breakfast for their pupils. The Patrician Brothers who arrived in 1827 to found their renowned Monastery School, known as the 'Old Mon', also opened their famous Breakfast Institute, which provided clothing as well as food for the hundreds of poor boys attending the school at Lombard Street.

Later, the Sisters of Mercy, who arrived in Galway town in 1840, as well as opening a school for girls, also became active in caring for the sick, especially during the Great Famine. Sadly, one of the very first entrants, young Christine Joyce of the Joyce family of Tara Hall, Mervue, lost her life in 1849 administering to cholera victims of the Great Famine.

All these relief agencies would not be sufficient, however, if a greater failure of the potato crop occurred than that in 1822.

GOVERNMENT and LOCAL INTERVENTION

Conscious of this fact, the government saw the need to install an early form of public welfare programme to cater for the increasing levels of destitution becoming evident in town and countryside. By 1838 an Act 'for the more Effective Relief of the Destitute Poor of Ireland', which enshrined the principle that local property must support local poverty, was enacted and 130 Poor Law Unions were established in Ireland to aid the destitute. These Unions were 'manageable' areas of destitution, roughly 20 miles in diameter and centred around the main market towns where a workhouse would be situated, to which the destitute, consisting of entire families if necessary, could be sent in times of famine and want.

Consequently, property owners and certain rent payers in each Union area were now obliged to pay a 'Poor Rate' ordered by local Grand Juries towards the maintenance of the destitute in their own Union workhouse. This was to be administered by a local Board of Guardians composed of at least two-thirds from among elected property owners and less than one-third of official members from local clergy and magistrates.

GALWAY WORKHOUSES

In all, ten Unions were envisaged for County Galway, and in 1845 the main ones included the Galway Union covering 179,541 acres with a population of 88,273, Loughrea 153,811 acres with 71,744, Ballinasloe 220,359 acres with 99,026, Tuam 192,369 acres with 74,974, Gort 106,886 acres with 43,543, and Clifden 191,426 acres with 33,465. The first workhouse, at Gort, built to hold 500 paupers, was opened on 11 December 1841, followed by Ballinasloe (1,000) in January 1842, Galway town (800) in March, while others came on stream in Loughrea, Tuam and subsequently in Portumna, Oughterard, Mountbellew and Glenamaddy (the latter in 1849).

All the workhouses were designed by George Wilkinson to an H-shaped plan with an extended central spar housing the entrance lodge, encompassed by recreational yards, and all surrounded by a high wall. Beds were only supplied in the hospital section. The inmates had to sleep on straw palliasses placed on wooden platforms a mere 12 inches from the floor. Dress consisted of rough grey frieze suits for the men and calico gowns and petticoats for the women. Within a few short years entire families were begging to gain entry to these institutions as the spectre of death stalked the land.

LANDFALL OF The GREAT FAMINE

Destitution was already a sad fact of life for many in Galway when the unthinkable happened and potato blight appeared in 1845 across the county. By then the potato was the most extensively cultivated Irish crop from two million acres or one-third of the tilled land of Ireland during the 1840s.

Phytophtora infestans, the potato blight fungus, originated in America in 1843, spread to Belgium in a potato consignment and borne by south-east winds appeared in County Galway, first making its appearance in Clifden in July 1845. Yet all seemed fine during that summer all along the western seaboard as countless lazy-beds filled with ripening potatoes created little patches of ordered greenery amid the maze of stone walls and stony fields. 'Lazy' is a misnomer when applied to these narrow cultivation ridges, for toil and sweat went into their making from the rocky landscapes of Connemara to the rich limestone soils of Annaghdown.

The lush greening of the potato stalks promised much just then, but unseen by human eyes the balmy south-east winds were bringing death from Europe. The dreaded blight spores alighted on the greening stalks, and by autumn the rotting vegetation was giving off a shocking stench as tubers blackened and died in their earthen beds. One can well imagine the fearful scene, enacted countless times on slope or sheltered valley, as frightened simple people rushed to open bed after bed and found jellied rot. The terrible smell of putrefaction indicated that up to 35 per cent of Galway's potato crop had rotted by the end of 1845 as families faced into a long winter with hunger never far away.

FOOD DEPOTS

With a national drop of over one-third of the potato crop for that year, food prices rose sharply towards the end of 1845, and as the Corn Laws levied heavy taxes on foreign foodstuffs entering Britain, the British Prime Minister, Sir Robert Peel, secretly purchased £185,000 worth of Indian corn (maize) from America to reduce the gathering distress in Ireland. To distribute this food from localised depots, a Relief Commission was set up by Peel in November 1845, with Sir Charles Trevelyan, assistant secretary to the Treasury, overseeing the work. Consequently, food was distributed at various places along the Connemara coastline through the auspices of the evolving coastguard service. Nevertheless, deaths recorded during the first famine year were 344 for Galway town and 3,849 for the county.

The following year, 1846, saw the true extent of the Famine unfold with practically the whole of the potato crop failing. A typical example of the reporting of the growing panic is seen in the *Galway Mercury* of 29 August 1846 which reported under the stark headline, 'The Potato Crop':

> *Our accounts from all parts of the country represent the potato crop as utterly destroyed. Mr John Murphy of Abbeygate-street, has called at this office to state that on Tuesday last, he had twenty-seven feet dug out of his land at Ballybane, and did not get one stone of sound potatoes, although on the Thursday before four-fifths of them were good. In truth, the failure is universal.*

The result was soon obvious with the death rate for the town during that year rising to 631, while that in the county reached 5,556 despite new efforts to stem the starvation tide. These consisted mainly of setting up local Relief Committees, 648 for the entire country, and in December, under the auspices of the local organisation, the first soup kitchen was set up in St Augustine Street in Galway town, because by then much of the population found it increasingly difficult to purchase other foodstuffs due to rising prices.

PUBLIC WORKS

What was needed initially was more employment, and while some landlords started their own work schemes such as drainage and especially boundary wall building, the main thrust of famine relief in March 1846 was the provision of public works. The local Grand Juries applied for government grants, the Board of Works vetted the schemes proposed, and successful work applicants were granted work tickets by the local Relief Committees.

Road works and drainage were the most common schemes. One was the construction of the massive dyke embankment and the new road leading to Terryland on the outskirts of Galway town, while in the western outskirts the exclusive Threadneedle Road still carries its sad famine construction title, Bóthar na Mine (Meal Road), because Indian meal was given in lieu of wages.

Although nearly £5 million was spent on relief works over the winter of 1846–7, the coldest weather in living memory only added to the disaster now unfolding as 'Black 47' dawned. By January, although over 500,000 were employed on relief work, another 400,000 starving workers were seeking employment for a daily wage of one shilling, when three times that amount was needed to feed a family.

Crime became rampant and Galway Jail saw the number of 'vagrants' imprisoned in 1844 increase from just three persons to nearly 500 in 1848, while the Bridewell in Clifden, built to hold 18 persons, now overflowed with 69 inmates. Jail was obviously preferable to starvation for an increasingly destitute population.

WORKHOUSES OVERFLOW

Obviously the workhouse system now bore the brunt of the expanding calamity when thousands of Irish families found themselves destitute as 1847 spread its early frosts across a famished western seaboard. Seed potatoes had been eaten by the starving lower classes, and the fishing tackle of the poorer fishing communities, such as the Claddagh fishing village, as well as hundreds of its famous Claddagh rings, had been pawned for food. By February 1847 the Poor Law system was beginning to collapse as thousands sought refuge in the country's 112 workhouses, already crammed to bursting point with 116,000 inmates.

Clifden had 800 (500 too many), but most pressure seemed to fall on the Galway town workhouse. Originally built to hold 800, it reached 1,302 in 1847 with many more clamouring for entry. In December 1847 it was reported that 313 paupers were seeking admission, but the workhouse was already overcrowded.

Meanwhile a store in Newtownsmyth was pushed into emergency use to accommodate between 300 and 400 children, as was Straw Lodge behind the workhouse. Auxiliary workhouses were commissioned in Dangan, at West House in St Helen's Street, and a corn store on Merchants Road was converted into another with accommodation for 1,000 people. During 1848 further auxiliary workhouses were commissioned at Barna and a temporary Fever Hospital at Moycullen was converted to an auxiliary workhouse especially for children.

SOUP KITCHENS

By March 1849 the total number of inmates in Galway town work-houses was 3,310. The situation was the same all along the western seaboard (Clifden Union used Bunowen Castle as an auxiliary work-house), but conditions would have been more desperate except for the passing of the 'Act for the Temporary Relief of Destitute Persons of Ireland' in February 1847 (the Soup Kitchen Act).

A new Relief Commission was founded and through this Act it proposed a two-fold approach through the Irish Poor Law system to deal with the Irish Famine. This entailed establishing temporary feeding facilities (soup kitchens) until September of that year to replace Relief Works and Outdoor Relief, i.e. instead of going into workhouses the destitute could stay in their homes and collect food. The problem now was that all this had to be financed from local rates—Irish property had to pay for Irish poverty. It was bound to fail.

The soup kitchen system took some time to implement, however, which caused great hardship to over 200,000 let go from the Public Workhouse programme by June of 1847. In July the Galway Union was feeding through its Soup Kitchen programme some 56,000 people, while in the county area Ballinasloe had 30,876, Clifden 24,403, Gort 35,523, Loughrea 24,625 and Tuam 49,864.

Meanwhile in the city area local voluntary relief was expanding in a valiant attempt to feed the starving thousands. Various records sum up one month's efforts in the fight against the ever-increasing disaster, when for May 1847 there were other soup kitchens operating in and about the city area, backing up the original one in St Augustine Street which fed 2,700 people daily. The Dominican Fathers from a two-boiler kitchen in the Claddagh fed 900, the Dominican Nuns in Taylor's Hill 2,200, the Presentation Nuns 600, the Mercy Nuns 900, the Patrician Brothers 1,000, while other soup stations operated at Bohermore, Menlo, Castlegar, Merlin Park, Murrough, and at Carrowbrowne from the Coady soup kitchen, now just a shed with a galvanised roof, off the Corraline Road.

'SOUP' WAR IN CONNEMARA

The distribution of soup took on another meaning in the Connemara area, when the Rev. Alexander Dallas founded his Irish Church Mission there with Protestant landlord backing from such as James H. Darcy, whereby his proselytising schools provided soup to hungry children of the 'enslaved tenantry'. He was following in the footsteps of earlier efforts to introduce the reformed faith, led by such ardent 'foot soldiers of the Second Reformation Movement' as Charles Seymore. By 1848 Connemara was soon filled with small mission stations, bible readers, orphanages and 'porridge schools'. In Letterfrack, however, James and Mary Ellis, two Quakers from Bradford in Yorkshire, had shown another way forward by setting up a properly run estate in 1847, paying honest wages for work done.

The Catholic response was intense with the Catholic Defence Organisation under William Wilberforce leading the devotional revolution in re-establishing the supremacy of the Catholic faith in these far western areas. The Mercy Order, the Third Order of the Franciscans, and the Christian Brothers who set up Letterfrack Industrial School all came and spread their undoubted influence, with the ardent backing of Archbishop John MacHale of Tuam. In effect there was no contest in this mini religious war, and by 1870 both religious streams were acting out what they preached in proper Christian unity.

EXTRA TOWN HELP

Back in Galway town extra aid came from various new sources. Walter Joyce of Mervue granted £1,000 to the Galway Relief Committee, and ships carrying foodstuffs from emigrant Dudley Persse in New York, as well as for the Society of Friends operating in the city area, landed their cargoes in the city docks to much fanfare. Combined with these the introduction of a new scheme called outdoor relief saw the worst of the famine begin to ease in Galway town, although conditions were still dreadful. Various parish priests reported the harrowing scenes: Fr Roche in St Patrick's parish noted five deaths a day; while Fr Peter Daly, who helped feed 2,000 people a day in his Rahoon parish, still reported 52 deaths per week there.

Conditions in the rural areas were even worse, especially in Connemara and surprisingly in those parishes east of Galway town, where much reliance on the potato crop was the leading factor, which saw the Annaghdown electoral division, for instance, recording a decrease from 3,392 to 1,819, a drop of nearly 50 per cent. By the end of 1847, 1,919 people had died in the town, while in the county the death toll had risen to 12,852, figures that really do not show, for various reasons (children's deaths not being recorded diligently), the true extent of the disaster.

OUTDOOR RELIEF

The spectre of death loomed large again across Ireland in 1848, with a near total collapse of the potato crop recorded for that year. Outdoor relief, once the soup kitchens closed down in September 1847, allowed the able-bodied to work and collect food for their families, instead of having them enter the local workhouse. By February 1848 over 455,000 were in receipt. The number had risen to 800,000 by June.

The system gradually broke down when local rates failed to cover the massive costs involved. Landowners and tradesmen in the towns across the county simply could not afford the rising rate in the pound to finance the schemes locally. With many Unions becoming 'distressed' and then bankrupt, including Galway, dozens of Boards of Guardians were dissolved for failure to strike proper rates and were replaced with officials such as Capt. Samuel Hillard in the Galway Union, followed by Major Patrick McKie, both of whom died within a year of taking office from famine-related diseases.

Sadly, other factors also led to the breakdown in the Outdoor Relief programme. Tenants occupying land over a quarter of an acre, according to an Act successfully guided through parliament by Galway MP, Sir William Gregory of Coole Park, were now debarred from obtaining help, and many left their holdings for the workhouse. And as landlords became responsible for paying rates for all those tenants who paid less than £4 in rent, 1848 saw the start of the eviction era in earnest, with thousands dispossessed and families left to die in hastily made shelters in bogs and ditches. In June of that year a road inspector had the melancholy task of having his crew bury 140 corpses found along a stretch of the road outside Clifden.

FAMINE DISEASES

Death along the roadsides became a familiar scene throughout the county, as the Famine took its fatal hold. Many of the clachans simply disappeared as their occupants were evicted on non-payment of rent, fled to the nearest workhouse, emigrated or died from starvation or disease.

Disease now killed more people than starvation. This came about as a result of thousands of people cramming into workhouses where bad sanitation and living conditions led to many dying from famine-induced diseases such as typhus and relapsing fever which were spread by body lice, while dysentery and even cholera spread from contaminated water sources.

In Galway, as elsewhere in the county, temporary accommodation in fever sheds was set up, while extra structures in Galway Workhouse augmented the fever hospital part of the complex. Nearby, beside the appropriately named Beggers' Bridge, the main County Fever Hospital, now part of the NUI, Galway Irish Centre for Human Rights complex, had accommodation for 40 patients, but more than 300 were treated during the height of the cholera crisis of 1848.

As the fever spread, one sees the admission figure of 239 to Loughrea Fever Hospital in 1846 rising to 1,842 in 1849 as being typical of what was happening throughout the county. While over 600 died in Galway town during the cholera outbreak, over 3,000 had perished from it in Ballinasloe by August 1848.

This heavy famine toll was reflected in a huge decline in the population of Connacht, which fell from 1,418,859 to 1,010,031 between 1841 and 1851, a loss of 408,828 people. While Galway showed the biggest decline of 118,514, its percentage decrease of 26.92 was the lowest in Connacht.

GALWAY TOWN WORK OPPORTUNITIES

An explanation for Galway's low percentage decrease arises from the fact that the population of Galway town itself actually increased from 17,275 in 1841 to 23,695 in 1851 despite recording nearly 10,000 deaths during the same period. The reason was obvious. Major employment opportunities outside of relief works arose in the city during the Famine, which was coming to an end in 1850 when a near normal potato harvest was secured.

The chief of these developments was the construction of the new university, which commenced in 1846 and was completed by 1848. Hundreds of workers were employed on this major contract for the time, and much-needed revenue was generated for over 400 Galway households.

Happily, when the university was completed, a large new civil engineering project got under way nearby with the construction of the Eglinton Canal, named after Lord Eglinton who came in 1851 to open a new street (which bears his name today) as well as this new development. Designed to give access from the sea to the lake, the work involved in constructing this massive project ensured that many families got much-needed help during the closing years of the Famine. Naturally, news of these work opportunities lured many from other outlying areas, leading paradoxically to an increase in the town's population in the middle of the Famine.

FAMINE GRAVES

For a million Irish people, however, there was no escape, and the many harrowing newspaper and eyewitness accounts of famine deaths sear the modern soul. People perished by the side of the road and ditch, their mouths green with grass and weed. Families prayed and died together, their little houses tossed in about them by neighbours fearful of the spread of disease.

Many were buried where they fell, while others interred their loved ones with simple crude stones, many of which still peep out at us today from disused graveyards as in the old section of the graveyard in Roscam on the eastern suburb of Galway town. Others, cast off in death as mere numbers from the nearby workhouse, found true rest at last in 'Bully Acres', from the Gaelic 'buile' (out of their heads). The best example in County Galway is the Famine Memorial Park in Ballinasloe.

Some found rest in vast communal famine pits such as Poll na Churtha (Hole of the Buried) in Oughterard, or are commemorated by specially designated burial areas as in Bushypark Church graveyard or under a simple mound in the old graveyard at Carrowbrowne. Others found their rest in quiet grassy corners inside workhouse walls, as in Mountbellew.

FAMINE AFTERMATH IN COUNTY GALWAY

By 1850, when the worst of the Great Famine was over, with a million people dead and a further million Irish hearts beating on foreign soil, a different Galway town and county faced into the second half of the nineteenth century. Connacht lost over a quarter of its population in the five previous terrible years, with Galway, Mayo and Sligo showing the highest death rates. County Galway was particularly affected with its population of 422,923 in 1841 dropping to only 298,564 in 1851.

Contrary to general belief, South Connemara as well as Aran with its poor land did not suffer depopulation as much as Oranmore, Claregalway and Annaghdown, an area which lost over 40 per cent of its population between 1841 and 1851. The outskirts of Galway paid a heavy price also with Rahoon parish losing 50 per cent of its 12,000 population of 1841, as did the Gort/Loughrea Union area, which lost 17,922 in the same ten-year period.

On the land the number of farms under five acres had been halved, while the demise of the landlord system had been set in motion when the non-payment of rent saw various landowners fall into debt. However, many of the County Galway landlords were saved from bankruptcy through the intervention of the Encumbered Estates Act of 1849, which allowed those ruined by the Famine, such as the Darcys in Connemara, to sell their estates without first having to pay off debts.

The Famine also led to the destruction of the old tenant way of farming, and the clachan/rundale system as well as the cottier class went into rapid decline. As a result, all through the western areas, as little villages were tumbled down by uncaring landlords or were simply deserted because of death or emigration, a terrible silence descended on the countryside. This silence echoed all the more in the coastal townlands of Connemara where whole Irish-speaking communities simply disappeared. Thus began the decline of the native language in the very strongholds, which gave it a future.

START Of MASS EMIGRATION FROM The WEST

One of the main changes wrought by the Great Famine was an increase in emigration, especially to America, the land of opportunity and freedom. For many, a last avenue of escape was provided by the dreaded 'coffin' emigration ships, which regularly left Galway Docks laden down with those paying their passage to America. Many sold their last possessions for their tickets, while others were funded by landlords such as the Thompsons of Salroc in North Connemara or through the agency of the Quaker Emigration Fund.

From the depths of destitution, misery and death two new aspects of emigration became apparent, which saw 37,600 people emigrate from the county between 1841 and 1851, with some 13,000 leaving through Galway port alone. One was chain migration, where one member of the family 'went ahead' and subsequently sent back earnings to bring out more of the family.

The 'American Wake' became a feature of the harsh lifestyle in countless little townlands throughout County Galway, especially in Connemara, as the second half of the nineteenth century progressed. Song, dance and music filled the air of the little household, to be replaced later by the tears of departure as the young boy or girl left behind their Irish childhood to begin a new life 'across the water' doing 'whatever God granted them'. Mass emigration had begun, and it was to last right down to the late twentieth century.

The cold harshness of pure statistics gleaned from census and other returns show that the population of the county dropped, mostly through emigration, from 298,564 to 195,149 between 1851 and 1901, while in the same period Galway town's population fell from 23,695 to 13,426. In all, 201,202 people emigrated from the county in that half-century, many through the harbour of Galway itself, but more often through Cobh, already becoming the port of tears for countless Irish emigrants.

Marketing such trips was widespread, as is evident in an advertisement placed in the *Galway Mercury* in January 1847 which noted: 'The splendid New Brig, *Alice*, of 500 tons burden will sail for New York on 12 January, wind and weather permitting from Galway Bay.'

The 'blurb' went on to advise that the vessel was fitted up in a superior manner and that each passenger would be supplied with one pound of meal or bread per day, according to an Act of Parliament, and 'an abundance of fuel and water'. There is more, of course, because we are told further that three more splendid sailing ships would sail each subsequent month, all 'first class vessels' whose experienced masters would pay every attention to the passengers during the voyage.

With such blatant and unchecked advertising, it is not surprising to learn of 25,000 deaths among those emigrating to Canada in one year, as exemplified in the case of the *Midas* which left Galway for New Brunswick in May 1847, which saw one in every ten of its passengers die in transit!

While many young emigrants were destined never to return, the second aspect of emigration saw these fresh emigrants send letters home, containing precious dollars in the form of the 'American cheque', while their parcels of old clothes reeked for weeks of 'boladh America' (the smell of America) from the secreted mothballs.

DEMISE of LANDLORDISM

When death and distress visited County Galway during the Great Famine, resulting in the eradication of countless tenant dwellings, another major change forged on the Galway landscape was the demise of the landed gentry, symbolised by the fall of the 'Big House'. A major reason for this change in rural landscapes was the Great Famine, when many estates became overburdened with debt from Poor Law Union rates, the non-payment of rent by impoverished tenants, and the frequently extravagant lifestyles of their owners.

In Connemara the change was complete. The vast estate of the Martins of over 192,000 acres was bought cheaply by the Law Life Assurance Society of London and eventually sold to Richard Berridge in 1872 for £230,000. Thus, did the descendants of a famous medieval Galway tribal family disappear from the rural landscape, which had nourished them for generations. Nearby, the Darcy lands, so synonymous with Clifden, also went the way of auction to the Eyres of Bath, while the Blakes of Renvyle sold their eastern lands to Mitchell Henry from Manchester, later MP for the district, who built the world-famous Kylemore Abbey of today as a wedding gift for his young wife.

Meanwhile, in the east of the county, landlords in debt could not avail of government investment loans or capital while suffering such encumbrances. The enactment of the Encumbered Estates Act of 1849 freed landlords from debt, allowing them to sell and repurchase part of their property. By April 1853 it was noted that total sales in County Galway came to over £1 million as compared to the national figure of nearly £9 million. As can be imagined, hundreds of transactions occurred as a result of this Act, and by 1916, 65 per cent owned the land they occupied, compared to only 3 per cent in 1870. Other agents came into play now, leading eventually to the final abolition of landlordism.

LAND AGITATION

After the Great Famine hearts hardened among survivors to the injustices of the prevailing land tenure system. Burdened with some guilt, a determination grew among them that Ireland should belong to the Irish and its land to the people. Thus, a two-strand approach to obtaining freedom of the country as well as land tenure was born.

While actual physical resistance had already manifested itself in County Galway during the Ribbonmen disturbances in the Sliabh Aughty region at the start of the nineteenth century, tenants became more involved in promoting agrarian revolt rather than armed aggression as proposed by the Irish Republican Brotherhood in the wake of the Famine.

Various factors brought the land question to the fore, not least the occurrence of further mini famines in 1866/7, 1873 and especially in 1879/80. However, progress in bringing equity to land tenure began to appear on the political front with the advent in 1868 of William Gladstone as a liberal Prime Minister with a 'justice for Ireland' theme as part of his election manifesto. Within a year he disestablished the Church of Ireland, thus relieving Catholic land users from paying the dreaded tithes. In 1870 he introduced a Land Act, the first of many seeking to redress the injustices of the Irish land ownership system. Best of all perhaps was the Ballot Act passed in 1872, allowing secret voting by a tenant, thus weakening even further the power of the landlord and his agent.

Meanwhile, another agent of change was quietly working away in the background from 1852 to 1866 under the direction of Sir Richard Griffith as the Griffith Valuation of buildings and land in particular was undertaken. It soon became apparent that rents being paid by the majority of tenants were excessive in the extreme. Rackrenting by unscrupulous landlords had become the norm, and now with statistical proof to hand, many led the way in seeking land reform in County Galway.

Chief among them was Bishop Patrick Duggan of Clonfert, who, in helping Captain Nolan defeat a landlord nominee in a parliamentary election in 1872, kindled the glowing embers of the fight for freedom of land tenure. Others rushed to join the battle.

Among them was Matt Harris, who later became MP for the Ballinasloe area after he helped form the Tenants' Defence Association there in 1876, which saw crowds of up to 5,000 attend rallies all over East Galway, paving the way for the founding of the Irish National Land League by Michael Davitt in 1879. Having been appointed organiser of this new national organisation in 1880, Harris helped form branches in such places as Athenry, Creggs, Gurteen, Mountbellew, Ballinasloe, Craughwell, Kiltullagh, Kilchreest, Killnadeema and Kilrickle.

While other famous names like Charles Stewart Parnell, James Dillon and William O'Brien shared the public limelight in the expanding Land War, the battle lines were already drawn when Hubert, the 2nd (and last) Marquis of Clanricarde, the largest landlord with some 56,826 acres in East Galway, raised his tenants' rent in retaliation for their backing of Nolan. Thus, the real engine of the agrarian revolution, the tenants themselves, formed Tenants' Defence Associations as well as Land League branches and became the vanguard in the land confrontations of the late nineteenth century.

Chief among these were the Woodford Tenants' Defence Association, which participated in one of the most famous stands against the battering ram and eviction at the home of Thomas Saunders in Woodford. Because of coverage by the press, the engagement became known as the Siege of Saunders' Fort when the landlord's force led by 700 police and including two companies of troops finally overcame 22 brave Woodford men defending the threatened homestead in August 1886. The press got its copy, but the Land War got the sweet oxygen of publicity it needed to embarrass the British Government into real action.

The PLAN of CAMPAIGN

This famous stand inspired fresh resistance leading to 'The Plan of Campaign' being initiated in the Woodford district, which spread across county and country. Organised on an estate basis, it consisted of offering a fairer rent to the local landlord and if refused, to pay it into a local central fund from which evicted families would be paid an allowance. Initially set in motion in a famous confrontation in Portumna on 18 November 1866, when 400 Clanricarde tenants collectively paid their refused rent offerings to national leaders Dillon and O'Brien, the campaign drew added strength from the encouragement offered by local clergymen, Rev. Patrick Coen and Rev. Patrick Egan, leading eventually to nearly 100 estates becoming involved.

Another welcome feature of the campaign saw evicted families offered shelter in specially built accommodation units. Ten huts were constructed in one day in the aftermath of evictions carried out on the estate of Sir Henry Burke of Marblehill. According to the *Western New and Weekly Examiner* of 13 February 1886, an estimated 10,000 persons came to house and cheer the evicted.

In time however due to funds running out and Clanricarde intransigence which saw 238 families evicted from his estate alone, many of those forced from their rented homes suffered deprivation for years to come, living in hardship and housed in cramped quarters by friends or in crumbling shacks beside the road.

But their sacrifice was not in vain, because by their actions and those of countless others, under such powerful political leaders as Davitt and Parnell world opinion, including the powerful emerging British working class, focused on the injustices of the landlord system in Ireland and forced the British Government into belated but welcome action.

Thus, County Galway played a major role in the Land War, which culminated in a plethora of Land Acts. That of 1881 saw the Land Commission set up, followed by the Congested Districts Board in 1891 which assisted nearly 60,000 applicants in acquiring their own holdings. With the famous Wyndham Act of 1903 enabling a further 250,000 to acquire their homesteads and a 1909 amendment making compulsory purchase possible, over 1.25 million acres were transferred to 400,000 'owner farmers'.

That the end of the ascendancy was nigh is evident in a short but pointed letter sent in 1904 by Clonbrock (one of Galway's most influential landed gentry) to a fellow landlord, Hyacinth D'Arcy of Newforest. It read simply: 'My dear D'Arcy, Pray make any use of my letter you like. I am afraid it can be of little service. I wish I could do more to help you. Sincerely, Clonbrock.'

Perhaps Mark Bence-Jones in his *Twilight of the Ascendancy* (1987) best sums up the final outcome with these words: 'To drive through County Galway is to follow a succession of crumbling demesne walls, with occasionally a ruined house half buried in ivy, though more often than not the house has, like Coole, been razed to the ground.' The ruins of Tyrone House near Clarinbridge bear out the truth of his statement.

FORMATION Of GALWAY COUNTY COUNCIL

By the end of the nineteenth century County Galway was entering a new and exciting phase of rural development as more and more owner farmers were enjoying the fruits of the division of landed estates and looking to modern agricultural techniques and associations to improve life on the land. In keeping with the changing times, reform of local government was also needed and it came when the Local Government Act of 1898 set up Galway County Council to replace the two Grand Juries of the town and county.

Meanwhile, Galway town merged back into the county as an urban district, having its own Urban District Council to run its affairs. Thus, complexities in local administration and revenue collection were greatly remedied with the stroke of a pen. For Galway City, however, the closing nineteenth century saw industrial stagnation set in, partly as a result of the Great Famine and, surprisingly, from the development of two new transport systems.

COMING Of The RAILWAY

The first development captured the imagination towards the end of the Great Famine. New railway lines were being opened and when Rahoon parish priest, Fr Peter Daly, first mooted a western branch to the Dublin line from Athlone via Ballinasloe and Athenry to Galway town, Connacht held its breath. This famous parish priest, and Galway City's greatest entrepreneur, who had the Lynch Memorial Window constructed in 1854 (thus presenting Galway with the world's first official tourist trap), saw yet another ambitious scheme commence when the first train of the Midland Great Western Railway finally trundled into Galway's new railway station in 1851. Passengers found ready accommodation in the adjoined and equally impressive Great Southern Hotel.

While much excitement was engendered with the joining of Dublin and Galway by rail link, despondency spread among Galway's industrial chiefs when low-priced foreign goods and equipment began to flood the home markets. What was a bonus for the travelling public became a nightmare for the local manufacturers as furniture, household goods and luxury items flowed into the terminus at Eyre Square for instant dispersal among the growing number of shops and bars in the city's streets.

Inevitably, local factory, distillery, brewery and mill closures followed as Galway's industrial boom gradually dissipated and emigration began its lonely call again. The sad ranks of these fresh emigrants were augmented by youths from the nearby fishing village of the Claddagh, jobless after powerful trawlers made fishing from the village's ancient hookers uneconomic and a waste of youthful energy. Learning English now became a necessity for those young Claddonians as they looked westwards to places called New York, Philadelphia and Boston.

TRANSATLANTIC LINES

As America beckoned, people were thrilled with Fr Daly's newest venture, the development of the town as a transatlantic port. In partnership with Manchester businessman, John Orrell Lever, he established the Atlantic Steam Navigation Company, known locally as the 'Galway Line', in 1858. In all, 16 commissioned ships, including the specially built paddle steamer *Connaught* (which was launched on Tyneside in April 1860 and sank on her second voyage to Boston), carried over 30,000 passengers before the company's closure in 1864.

'An over-ambitious and ultimately incompetent management who offered a service to the public before suitable ships were ready' was the main reason for the company's demise according to Timothy Collins, a leading Galway maritime historian. Although having lost half its fleet to the cold Atlantic, the company, in priding itself on never losing a passenger, failed to mention the fate of the crews!

A heavy loss was incurred by investors and the closure of the line stifled further capital ventures by the Galway business community. Emigration increased even further as a result, especially in the wake of some harsh winters in the late 1870s, followed by another serious famine in 1879.

Unlike the 1845–50 disaster, however, a proper transatlantic service became available when the Canadian-based Allan Shipping Line commenced operations between Galway and the land of opportunity in 1880. Town and county provided passengers for the steerage section of the first ship of the line, the *Austrian*, when she left Galway Bay on 11 June of that year. Also on board were 50 families from Connemara and South Mayo, eager to start a new life on virgin land waiting for them in Minnesota, provided they left behind 'the practice of making poteen'! By the time the Allan Line made its last Galway call in 1905 it had averaged about 30 visits a year, as the little town of Cobh became the hub of emigration—a stark reminder of what the West had lost.

Galway had to wait until 5 May 1928 to have the next permanent transatlantic service commence again, when the SS *Muenchen* called and inaugurated a service which ceased only when the world went to war in 1939. Prior to that up to four liners per week lit Galway Bay at night as the local tender ferried up to 700 passengers weekly between ship and shore.

After the war, the Holland-American Line restarted a transatlantic service, which lasted for a number of years, with the harbour authority constructing a passenger transit shed on the newly extended dock pier to cater for passengers. It was not to be, however, as costs and the lack of actual shore docking facilities for these giant ships ended this fourth attempt at establishing a permanent Galway transatlantic link. Today only one or two luxury liners call annually to Galway Bay as the city reflects yet again on what might have been, or perhaps still might be.

TOWNS AT END Of The 19TH CENTURY

As the twentieth century dawned, stagnation was evident in the main county towns. Tuam, a Corporation town, ranked second to Galway as a trading centre and with a population of 6,883 in 1837, should have progressed when its Corporation was abolished in 1840 and new Town Commissioners elected in 1843. But the inability to strike rates, which the Commissioners as large property owners would mostly have had to pay themselves, stymied any real progress and the town population decreased to 4,223 by 1871.

When the Local Government Act of 1898 created Galway County Council, the local Tuam board refused to become an Urban District Council mainly because of the rates issue, staying merely, according to Galway County Council historian Gabriel O'Connor, as 'contractors' for Galway County Council. The legacy of once hosting the High Kings of Ireland had long since passed and only Tuam's religious ambience, embellished by the consecration of its magnificent cathedral in 1836, marked its presence in County Galway.

Athenry, the other Corporation town with Galway, was already much reduced by strife and war through the ages, so that by 1856 'its houses and shops were poor, the streets unpaved, its Tuesday market had long since vanished and its three fairs poorly attended'. With only 1,487 inhabitants in 1851, Athenry never fulfilled the dreams of its founding fathers, the de Berminghams, all those years ago.

Loughrea was in decline also during the latter half of the nineteenth century, with its population dropping to 2,557 in 1901 from 3,681 in 1851 as the influence of its proprietors, the Earls of Clanricarde, waned. Like Galway, its brewery, tanneries and corn mills felt the chills of economic competition, even though the arrival of the railway branch line from Attymon Junction, as well as the building of its magnificent cathedral at the start of the twentieth century, brought some hope and pride.

Gort was described as a market and post town in 1837 by Samuel Lewis. Composed of 563 houses and containing a population of 3,627, it had a substantial flour mill constructed in 1806, a courthouse erected in 1815 and two churches. However, it went into decline following the Great Famine and the subsequent building of its railway station as part of the Limerick/Tuam railway link, which saw cheap goods eventually flood the home market.

Ballinasloe, on the other hand, was described as one of the most flourishing towns in Ireland under the management of the Trench family in the nearby estate at Garbally. Farming and its ancillary industries and crafts had prospered, as exemplified by the activities of the Ballinasloe Horticultural Society, founded in 1833, and in the size and good will engendered by its famous annual fair to which the railway station played an important part in transporting live animals from all over Ireland. Linked also to the Shannon by canal via the River Suck, its industries flourished during the nineteenth century, and with a population of 5,169 by 1911, looked to the future as its Urban District Council garnered rates of £11,000 p.a. for its town services.

Clifden too, through much petitioning for funds, thrived initially after its foundation by John D'Arcy in the early years of the nineteenth century, and thrilled to the words of Daniel O'Connell when he addressed one of his 'Monster Repeal Meetings' there on 13 September 1843. The sudden death of its founder in 1839 and the advent of the Great Famine dulled its growth, however, but the construction of the Galway/Clifden railway line in 1895 (it closed in 1935) offered fresh hope from the tourism and fishery aspects for this former seaport as the nineteenth century ended, as did the town's popular Connemara Pony Show.

All these towns including smaller ones stagnated with the various depressions of the twentieth century, but profited towards the end with the effects of the economic upturn of the Celtic Tiger. Many have thrived with the success of Galway City; those nearer to it gained from rising property prices and transport access. Some like Clifden found international acclaim from Marconi's radio station or the crash landing of Alcock and Browne on their doorstep in 1919 after the world's first east/west transatlantic flight; Tuam benefited, as did the farmers in its region, from its sugar beet industry from 1934 until the factory's demise in 1987; Glenamaddy from its dance music days of the 1960s and 70s; Spiddal from its Gaeltarra Éireann industries; Portumna from its River Shannon tourist traffic; Milltown from its continuous success as Galway's 'tidiest town', not forgetting its favourite son, playwright M.J. Molloy; Athenry from its medieval festivals; as did many other rural areas from sport, festivals and even novenas.

SURGE TO NATIONHOOD

It could be argued that the Great Famine was the nineteenth-century catalyst which shook the nation from its colonial minion status and began a tidal surge towards nationhood. A tide comes in many waves, however, and as the nineteenth century drew to a close there were many of an Irish nationalistic intent breaking on the English shore. The passive fight for Irish tenure of Irish land was one such wave, and when it beached with victory, others followed in its foaming wake. Catholic resurgence was another surging wave.

CATHOLIC RESURGENCE

Catholic Emancipation, achieved in 1829, and previous Catholic Relief Acts laid the foundation of a devotional revolution of the native faith that swept Ireland in the early decades of the nineteenth century. A building boom in churches resulted, and crucially in the Galway context, the old wardenship (the Catholic as distinct from the Protestant) which had given Pope Gregory XVI 'more trouble than all Ireland put together while it was under the spiritual direction of a warden' was abolished. Fr George Browne was consecrated the first Bishop of the new Galway diocese, the youngest in the country, on 23 October 1831, which saw Kilmacduagh and Kilfenora added to it in 1883.

Today the Galway diocese forms a crescent around the city, its rural parishes consisting of Ennistymon, Kilfenora, Liscannor, Lisdoonvarna/ Kilshanny, Ballyvaughan, Carron/New Quay, Kinvara, Gort, Beagh, Kilbeacanty, Peterswell, Kilchreest, Ardrahan, Ballinderreen, Clarinbridge, Craughwell, Oranmore, Claregalway, Castlegar, Barna, Moycullen, Spiddal, Killanin, Oughterard, Rosmuc, Lettermore, and Shrule, an outlier in County Mayo. At present 72 churches serve the diocese. The parish chapel in Middle Street in Galway town, which had become the Pro-Cathedral in 1831, was decommissioned in 1965 with the opening of the new cathedral in that same year.

Tuam diocese includes the rest of Connemara and, rather surprisingly, the Aran Islands, as well as the northern portion of County Galway, while the diocese of Clonfert incorporates much of the eastern section of the county with treasured Loughrea Cathedral as its base.

Ironically, one outcome of the Great Famine saw the institutional Church become firmly established, leading to the gradual demise of many of the ancient pilgrimages to patterns and holy wells. Parishes became better organised, each seeking in time to build its own church, while Religious Orders also came to play a very important part in education affairs, especially after the Education Act of 1831 saw the commencement of the National School system.

In time many secondary schools were founded by the Orders: St Mary's College opened its doors in 1912 as the diocesan college for the Galway diocese; Garbally for Clonfert in 1923; and St Jarlath's for Tuam in 1858.

A feature of this 'devotional revolution' however was the calibre of its leaders such as the Archbishop of Tuam, John MacHale (1791–1881), who was the dominant figure in Galway for decades and who fought fearlessly for the Repeal of the Union, Catholic Emancipation, the abolition of tithes and, above all, tenants' rights. Described as the 'Lion of the Fold of Judah' by Daniel O'Connell, MacHale epitomised the new calibre of these church leaders right down to Dr Michael Browne, Bishop of Galway, who saw the opening of Galway Cathedral in 1965 as the greatest achievement of his episcopacy. Thus the surge to nationhood had religious leaders, not only it seemed with God on their side, but the courage to express forcibly the wishes of a native flock bowed for so long by history itself.

IRISH CULTURAL REVIVAL — The LANGUAGE

This gathering surge to nationhood would founder, however, if an Irish cultural wave failed to surface from the depths of a recent gloomy past and come crashing ashore on the exposed flanks of 'perfidious Albion'. The core of such a cultural move would be the Gaelic language, which after the Great Famine was a fading widow in much of the western seaboard and a simple cadaver in the teeming alleyways of Irish Victorian urbanity.

Yet there was more than a murmur left in the sean-bhean bocht because the Gaelic outpourings of the poet Antaine Ó Raifteirí in his early nineteenth-century wanderings along the winding roads about Craughwell were an inspiration to the Gaelic League founded in 1893 by Douglas Hyde specifically to preserve the language.

Less than a century later another traveller of the winding Galway roads, this time with his little black donkey and cart, would take the lead in an Irish language crusade and leave an imprint, deep even by today's standards. Between his birth in Galway City in 1882 and his death in

Dublin in 1928, Pádraic Ó Conaire, whose delightful stone statue by Albert Power graced Eyre Square until 2004, left a rich corpus of Irish literature comprising hundreds of essays, articles, short stories and books to feed the growing appetite of a later cadre of Gaelic writers such as Máirtín Ó Cadhain (1916–73) of Cois Fharraige and Máirtín Ó Direáin (1910–88) from the Aran Islands.

Promoting the native tongue was another passive but powerful weapon in the surge towards nationhood. It found gathering favour especially with Pádraic Pearse, the leader of the 1916 Rising in Dublin, who discovered a haven of Gaelic inspiration in his little Connemara cottage at Rosmuc. When Galway County Council substituted Gaelic for the former English signage on its new milestones around Ballinasloe in 1903, it was another indication that the cultural surge was gathering strength, as more waves rushed to feed the flow.

MUSIC

The arts too found revival in the awakening soul of Irish culture, when the Gaelic League organised the first Oireachtas Festival in 1897, which catered for Irish music, song and literature, while in 1896 the first Feis Ceoil to promote Irish music especially, was co-founded by dramatist and wealthy Catholic landlord, Edward Martyn of Tullira Castle near Gort.

Now native music, song, dance and literature had a national platform for excellence, and competition became intense to achieve national awards, which brought honour, not only to the winning participants, but to the locality they represented. Typical of this was when 'enthusiasts' took blind piper, Martin Reilly, who had fallen on hard times, from the Gort workhouse to participate in the Pipers' Festival at the annual feis in the Rotunda in Dublin, where he won first prize despite being out of practice for so long. In Galway, by 1918 the West had its own Feis Chonnacht, which by 1936 had become the Feis Ceoil an Iarthair. Later musical groups such as the Ballinakill Ceilí band ensured that traditional sounds never went away, as do Maighe Seola, who were formed in 1997 and have been performing the old songs sung around Tuam, which were collected by Eibhlin Bean Mhic Choistealbha in the early 1900s. With the likes of singers Dolores and Seán Keane, musician Frankie

Gavin and the Saw Doctors from Tuam, music is very much alive in County Galway today.

At the start of the twentieth century, therefore, a subtle change was becoming evident in the mindset of the ordinary people—one could have pride now in one's native cultural activity, which after all was based on a long-lost Celtic past. Now as one listened to the uileann pipes or a sean nós singer or watched a tap dancer, you could almost sense if not taste that unique past when Ireland was a separate nation. The message was becoming clear—it could be so again.

THEATRE

A national theatre opened in Dublin in 1899, but for its roots one must look westwards to a meeting at Doorus House, Kinvara, between Lady Gregory, W. B. Yeats and Edward Martyn some months earlier, when the idea of an Irish Literary Theatre was first mooted. Thus did the Abbey Theatre eventually play its part upon the larger stage of the Celtic Revival sweeping the country at the time, underpinning even further the surge towards achieving national identity.

At home in Galway City, however, the ultimate dream of a pure Gaelic theatre, where only Irish would be used in plays and sketches, was achieved when a group of academics under Dr Séamus Ó Beirn founded Taibhdhearc na Gaillimhe, which opened its doors on 27 August 1928 to a production of Mícheál Mac Liammóir's *Diarmuid agus Gráinne*. An *Irish Independent* report, according to local theatre expert Seán Stafford, underlined the importance of the event with these stirring words: 'A Gaelic Theatre in Ireland that will be able to compete with the Theatre in English, in London or the Theatre in French, in Paris, is the ideal of the committee of the new Gaelic Theatre in Galway in which the first performance was given last night.' On the boards, at least in Galway City, Ireland had become a nation.

LITERATURE

A few miles to the south a giant copper beech tree stands as a silent, natural icon to another early twentieth-century Renaissance faction of the arts in Galway, for the initials it bears on its ageing bark record the gathering of the giants of Irish literature, who 'came like swallows' to Coole Park, the home of Lady Isabella (Augusta) Gregory and head-quarters of the Irish Literary Revival. Here this co-founder of the Abbey Theatre offered a tranquil retreat for the literary elite of her day, providing fresh opportunities for the likes of W. B. Yeats, George Bernard Shaw, Seán O'Casey, John Millington Synge (who had already produced his famous work, *The Playboy of the Western World*, after his sojourn earlier on the Aran Islands) and a host of others to find fresh inspiration among the woody bowers of Coole.

So entranced was Yeats with Coole, as well as with nearby Tullira Castle, the home of Edward Martyn, that he felt compelled to purchase, repair and dwell in a famous castle, the Tower House of Ballylee, where this leader of the Irish Literary Revival and winner of the Nobel Prize for Literature in 1923 resided for many years, composing perhaps much of *The Tower*, considered to be among his best collection of poems.

Lady Gregory, for her part, inspired by Yeats, became an avid writer and collector of folklore from the gentle rural commonalty about her, a playwright specialising in one-act comedies and, after learning Irish, an important translator, especially of ancient Irish epics. The spirit of Cuchulain went forth among the Irish again, thanks to the literary efforts of this inspirational patron of the arts as the new century got into its stride.

Just then in Galway City young Nora Barnacle was planning to widen her meagre prospects and go to Dublin, and perhaps meet the man of her dreams. She did, of course, and when she and James Joyce dallied in each other's company on that fateful Bloomsday of 16 June 1904, English literature would, in time, acknowledge the inspirational influence a simple working-class girl from Galway would have on the world's greatest prose writer of the twentieth century.

VISUAL ARTS

Except for artist Joseph Patrick Haverty, who was born in Galway City in 1794 and became noted for his painting of Pádraig Ó Bhrian, the blind Limerick piper, which was sold in the November 2003 auction of the contents of Lissadell House, native art in its many forms found little expression except in a few of the parish churches being built in the nineteenth century. All that changed, however, when in 1897 St Brendan's Cathedral began to rise over Loughrea and became the greatest repository in Ireland dedicated to the revival of Celtic Art in its stained glass, stone, wood and metalworks, wrought by the leading artists and craftsmen of the time.

Inspired by the aforementioned Edward Martyn of Tullira and supervised by building secretary, Fr Gerald O'Donovan, this beautiful cathedral became a template for the Irish Catholic Church in its Irish Revival building programmes. It became a treasure-house of excellence promoting the first stained-glass windows to be produced in the Sarah Purser school, An Túr Gloine (The Tower of Glass) Co-operative, in 1903. The cathedral now includes works by Purser, Child, Healy and Hone, marble and bronze from John Hughes, stonework by Michael Shortall, banners by Jack B. Yeats, and the furnishings by architect William A. Scott.

Of interest is the fact that William A. Scott went on to design the parish church of Spiddal, which opened in 1908, a feature of which are the Stations of the Cross, designed by Túr Gloine, which consist of a mosaic of painted glass, reflecting again the new superiority of Irish craftsmanship over previously imported church materials. Meanwhile in St Michael's Church in Ballinasloe, the finest Celtic Renaissance in metalwork can be seen on the tabernacle by Mia Cranwell.

Commenting on this revolution in Irish craftsmanship, which is clearly seen in the windows of Labane Church, Dr Peter Harbison, a leading expert on ecclesiastical art and heritage, describes the stained-glass work of the Túr Gloine group and Harry Clarke as Ireland's greatest contribution to European art in the twentieth century. Like the Irish Literary Theatre, this unique Irish stained-glass movement found its origin stirred and certainly shaken into life by what can best be described as the 'Galway connection'.

The GAA

Parity in so many facets of Irish life, combined with a growing distinctiveness as evidenced in the growth of the Gaelic Athletic Association (GAA), providing an official platform to play one's national games of hurling and Gaelic football at the highest level, engendered a growing sense of national confidence in the Irish psyche. Here again

County Galway played a pivotal role in the development of the GAA. While hurling 'with the little ball' had been banned by a Galway Corporation Act of 1527, the game flourished in the countryside, with Killimor and Meelick leading the way.

From the Galway perspective, the first convention of the GAA there was held in Athenry on 24 October 1886; the first 'Interprovincial' hurling match took place between Kilmacduagh (Co. Galway), the winners, and Carron (Co. Clare) in Boston, Co. Clare, on 28 November 1886; while the first All-Ireland took place on 1 April 1888 in Birr, with Meelick representing Galway losing to Thurles (Co. Tipperary).

With Gaelic football also becoming popular (4,000 spectators attended a football match in January 1886 between Leitrim and Mullagh), in time Galway would become one of the leading GAA counties in Ireland, winning All-Ireland Senior finals in hurling in 1923, 1980, 1987 and 1988, while football titles came in 1925, 1934, 1938, 1956, 1964–66, 1998 and 2001. Today every parish in the county has a playing pitch, with major stadiums in Tuam, Ballinasloe, Athenry and Loughrea, culminating with the reopening of Pearse Stadium in Galway City in 2003. A recent feature is the involvement of women in these two sports, with success coming to the senior county camogie players in 1996.

Meanwhile, at the end of the nineteenth century, GAA players were obvious candidates for enlistment in the Irish Republican Brotherhood, founded in 1895 to promulgate a more militant campaign to achieve Irish freedom. The surge towards nationhood was now entering a more dangerous phase as land tenure politics gave way to those of a purely nationalist nature.

FIGHT FOR INDEPENDENCE

The Irish Party, formed in 1874 to soldier politically first for Home Rule, barely survived a split following the scandal involving its leader Charles Stewart Parnell, but was reunited under John Redmond. An inevitable split occurred again in the newly formed Irish Volunteers, an extension of the IRB, when Redmond called on all nationalists to support the British war effort in the First World War to ensure Home Rule when the conflict ended. While many Volunteers joined the British Army as a result, the rest saw armed struggle as the only guaranteed way to an independent Ireland.

All the latter needed was proper organisation, and in Galway this was provided by Liam Mellows, who was appointed provincial instructor at the Volunteer Convention in 1914, with his base at Athenry. In just two years the fruit of his work was tested by the national Easter Rising of 1916, which started in Dublin, when he led over 700 men in Galway's rebellion to gain control of the eastern section of the county. It was a premature attempt, however, for countermanding orders aborted it within a few days and the only western rising fizzled out in some confusion.

While no executions followed in County Galway, imprisonment strengthened resistance even more in its Volunteers on their release in 1917. Reorganisation, initially under OC Larry Lardner and then under Seamus Murphy, had the insurgents divided into four brigades, West Connemara with Peter McDonnell as OC, East Connemara, Micheál Ó Droighneáin OC, North West had first Con Fogarty and then Paddy Donleavy as OC, South East, Laurence Kelly OC, while Galway City had a separate unit under Seamus Murphy, later replaced by Seán Broderick.

The die was cast now, and up to the signing of the Truce in December 1921, Galway contributed much to the Fight for Independence, with attacks on police barracks at Castlehacket, Barna and Loughgeorge initiating the campaign in the first months of 1920. When three policemen were killed in ambushes outside Mountbellew and Tuam in July, the first of the terrible retributions by Crown forces, spearheaded by the feared Black and Tans, occurred when Tuam Town Hall was burned down and many buildings damaged by fire, bullets and bombs, a scene revisited on Clifden, Gort, Oranmore, Headford, and many of the smaller towns and villages in the county.

Dozens of people lost their lives in these pogroms, including Fr Michael Griffin and Councillor Michael Walsh in Galway City, while the murder of Mrs Ellen Quinn of Kiltartan and the Loughnane brothers from Shanaglish were particularly brutal. Thus, when a notice flashed across the screen in the Town Hall Cinema in Galway on the evening of 15 July 1921, announcing an Anglo/Irish Truce, the long agony of foreign occupation of County Galway had come to an end.

However, the terms of the treaty were rejected by the likes of Thomas 'Babs' Duggan from Roscam who, after taking over command of

Renmore Barracks when it was vacated by the British in 1922, tried to burn it down on joining the Anti-Treaty side shortly afterwards! Inevitably the civil war in County Galway consisted mostly of minor skirmishes before peace finally permeated the Corrib lands in 1923, with the Treaty side gaining complete control. The question now was whether city and county could look to economic recovery and even growth.

ECONOMIC RECOVERY — GALWAY CITY

Although the population of Galway City had fallen to 14,000 at the start of the twentieth century and its industry reduced to three mills and a foundry, there were encouraging signs of a recovery on many fronts. Already the Dún Aengus Dock, a new deep-water berth constructed by the Harbour Commissioners in 1883, was hosting a new steamer service operated by the Limerick Steamship Company.

Thanks to increased traffic into the port, imported coal, fertiliser and timber encouraged energetic entrepreneurs from the McDonogh and Hynes families to open vast dockland stores, fertiliser industries and hardware shops to cater for the increasing trade from new farming interests arising from the re-allotments of land and the arrival of local and national government agencies. Fresh retail interests opened along Shop Street as Galway began to stake its claim to become the capital of Connacht, a claim reinforced when King Edward VII paid a royal visit to the city in 1903.

It was also to become the administrative centre of the county, when Galway County Council located its headquarters in the former County Infirmary building on Prospect Hill in 1925.

Meanwhile, Galway Urban District Council was busy promoting new electricity sources, establishing waterworks at Terryland, and providing extra local housing facilities, as in the Claddagh where it replaced the old familiar thatched variety with a new estate of two-storey houses complete with gardens. The main aim of the Council, however, was to seek Corporation status again, and an Act was passed in 1937 reconstituting Galway as a borough. Its first mayor in 96 years was John F. Costelloe, who held this position until 1950.

In the meantime, a new and powerful ally in promoting Galway as a commercial and industrial base came on the scene in 1923 in the shape of the Galway Chamber of Commerce and Industry, a continuation of the Royal Galway Institution, which had originated as the Amicable Literary Society in 1791. However, initial success by the Chamber in establishing industries in the 1930s ranging from chemical works to the manufacture of ladies' hats was halted by the start of the Second World War, which saw survivors from the torpedoed passenger ship, the *Athenia*, brought ashore at Galway docks in September 1939 during the very first days of the conflict.

Wars and their effects lasted into the 1950s, and by 1951 an appeal for a £20,000 'start-up' industrial fund for the promotion of new industries by the Chamber was successful. Funds were allocated for the establishment of the Royal Tara China factory in Mervue and later for the purchase of six acres of land nearby to site Galway's first industrial estate, which through the agency of the Industrial Development Authority (IDA) and Galway Corporation, came to fruition in 1967, thus initiating the city's drive to establish a proper industrial base capable of future expansion.

Today, thanks to major harbour improvements carried out in the 1960s by the Harbour Board (now Galway Harbour Company), a new airport at Carnmore, and help and encouragement from such state bodies as the IDA, FÁS, Enterprise Ireland, and Ireland West, Galway had (2002) become a thriving city of 65,774 inhabitants with networks of housing, industrial, service and retail estates expanding yearly in its suburbs. Of great importance was its nomination as a gateway (the engine of growth) for Counties Galway, Mayo and Roscommon, supported by the linked hubs of Castlebar/Ballina and Tuam in the new National Spatial Strategy, with a projected 181,000 population in the city and its hinterland by 2020. Its international core of industrial firms provides most of its employment, with workers from the county commuting daily along improving but congested roads, which once led only to the emigration ship.

Much of this success is a tribute to a well-educated workforce, augmented greatly by the founding of Galway Regional Technical College in 1972. Re-titled the Galway/Mayo Institute of Technology (GMIT) in 1998, it provides with the ever-expanding National University of Ireland, Galway (NUI, Galway), a steady stream of third-level graduates conversant with the needs of modern industry and the knowledge society.

COUNTY GALWAY — HEALTH CARE

With the signing of the Anglo-Irish Treaty in 1921, the county faced into an uncertain future economically, but encouraged at least by the fact that its fate rested solely in Irish hands now, with the local government acting more and more, according to Gabriel O'Connor, as an agency of central government. The 1925 Act made the Council the rating authority for raising sums necessary to run the County Board of Health and Public Assistance, the Mental Hospital Committee and the Committee of Agriculture, as well as road maintenance and sanitary affairs.

When the County Infirmary facility transferred to the Galway Workhouse in 1922 and became the Central Hospital to replace all Union hospitals except Clifden, the vacated premises on Prospect Hill became the headquarters of the Council until it was demolished in 1997 and replaced by the present building. Meanwhile, a county home for the old and infirm was established in Loughrea Workhouse. With the County Management Act of 1940, the functions of the County Board of Health were transferred to the county manager, a system which lasted until 1970 when the Health Act of that year established Health Boards. The Western Health Board came into operation on 1 April 1971.

A feature of medical care in the early years of the new Irish state was the specialist treatment needed for tuberculosis, which saw the Woodlands facility opened in Renmore in 1924. (Merlin Park replaced it in 1952.) Toghermore Rehabilitation Centre, meanwhile, opened in Tuam in 1949.

Other major hospital buildings included the construction of the new Regional Hospital in 1956 on the old workhouse site, which was renamed University College Hospital Galway in 1989 because of its long association as a training hospital with the university. Meanwhile other hospitals were opened by Religious Orders such as Portiuncula in Ballinasloe in 1945 by the Franciscan Missionary Sisters, the Bon Secours in Tuam by the Bon Secours Sisters also in 1945, and who also opened Calvary Hospital in Galway in 1953.

COUNTY HOUSING

Providing housing was an important function of the County Board of Health with 1,332 labourers' cottages being provided between 1922 and 1946. Ironically, because of the economic boom towards the end of the century, house building restrictions on environmental protection grounds were introduced into the county by 2003.

Already, areas such as the coast road west from Galway City have been blighted by ribbon housing developments, leading to severe traffic congestion, prompting such measures as 'once off' housing, building restrictions within 15 km of Galway City, and in 2003 restricting house buyers to only Gaelic-speaking families in selected Gaeltact areas of Connemara in order to preserve the language.

COUNTY EDUCATION

Education improved at all levels in County Galway during the twentieth century. Religious Orders initially provided the post-primary tier needed, until the Vocational Education Act of 1930 introduced Vocational Schools to all the main towns of County Galway, with Glenamaddy one of the last to have a facility opened in 1965.

Comprehensive education at post-primary level was introduced in 1966 and free education and transport the following year, which were vital to the subsequent development of the county. Meanwhile Coláiste Éinde was founded in Salthill as a preparatory all-Irish language school in 1928, with the majority of pupils graduating to St Patrick's College, Drumcondra, Dublin, to train as primary school teachers.

Third-level education was broadened with the foundation of the Galway Regional Technical College in 1972. Falling religious vocations are a sign of the times, however, and the college recently acquired nearby Cluain Mhuire, the former Redemptorist seminary, as a base to house its Humanities faculty, as well as the disused Christian Brothers' reformatory school site at Letterfrack to establish a furniture design centre.

The importance of education in the agricultural sector was also recognised. Agricultural colleges were established in Athenry and Mountbellew, the latter now an outreach centre for the GMIT. The recent trend of vacating the land for the cities as small-scale farming becomes more and more non-viable demands that the latest knowledge, management and production techniques are available to those who remain in a rural business dominated by the Common Agricultural Policy, spatial strategies, and the need for protecting the environment as espoused by the Rural Environmental Protection Scheme and County Development Plans.

GAELTACHT

County Galway hosts one of the largest Gaeltachts, or mostly Irish-speaking areas in Ireland today, an area known as Cois Fharraige, stretching approximately from Barna to Carraroe in South Connemara. Various state agencies have been centred to nourish and maintain the language in this area, such as Roinn na Gaeltachta in 1956, followed a year later by Gaeltarra Éireann, which was quite successful in promoting industry, while Údarás na Gaeltachta (the Gaeltacht Authority) set up in 1980 gave a democratic voice to local residents.

However, the vernacular language continues to decline, and a Gaeltacht Commission in 2000 revealed that of 18 electoral districts with 75 per cent daily speakers of Irish, 12 are situated in County Galway. Modernity is coming to the rescue, however, with the establishment of Raidió na Gaeltachta at Costelloe in 1972, and also the siting of Teilifís na Gaeilge (TG4 today) at Ballinahown in 1996, while NUI, Galway is expanding university courses through Irish into Gaeltacht centres.

Even more influential in the general sense, it seems, is *Ros na Rún*, a television series in the 'soap opera' mould, which boasts the lilt of a Connemara Irish soundtrack and is now becoming popular with the younger set, the future custodians of the language.

GALWAY CITY TODAY

Today, confidence based on successful City Council Development Plans permeates the ancient narrow inner streets of Galway City and also the throbbing arteries of industry and the large shopping malls in its ever-widening peripheries. The barometer of this success can be confirmed in the rising spiral of Galway property prices (second only to Dublin) or in the number of construction cranes on city skylines, as well as in the many cafés, restaurants and pubs filled with an affluent younger generation.

While industrial and commercial factors have played a major role in this success, location has contributed also to this economic showcase which is Galway today. Despite mini recessions in the 1950s and 1970s, Galway City on river and bay, as well as being a gateway to Connemara, the Burren and the Aran Islands, has been next only to Dublin and Killarney in the tourist trail of Ireland.

The city itself has become a major tourist attraction, thanks mainly to its 1984 quincentennial celebrations of 500 years of mayoralty, as well as its unchanged medieval street plan, enhanced by the various urban renewal schemes carried out in recent times in special tax-designated areas. Revitalisation requires that ancient buildings or portions of them are to be conserved within new developments, and to include retail or office accommodation at ground level and living accommodation in upper storeys.

A typical development is the Eyre Square Shopping Centre, with two levels of shops, a car parking facility, and an upper level of apartments, while at the same time its important portion of the medieval town wall, complete with two towers, has been restored and conserved. Erected initially to keep strangers out, the wall is now a tourist attraction enticing visitors to come and enjoy the blend of the new and the old in a modern shopping ambience.

To underline the growing prestige of this ancient City of the Tribes, important visitors in recent times have included Presidents of the United States (John F. Kennedy 1963, Ronald Reagan 1984) and Pope John Paul II in 1979. While pedestrianisation of the medieval heart of the city and a winding waterways walk have been new attractions for native and tourist alike, Galway also delights in its new-found fame as the festival capital of Ireland.

As well as its long-established Galway Races, new events such as its renowned Arts Festival, including on-street performances by the Macnas theatrical group, the International Oyster Festival, Film Fleadh, and Cúirt International Poetry Festival, augmented by sell-out performances of its Tony Award-winning Druid Theatre, are some of the events which combine to place Galway at the top of the auctioneer's portfolio.

The ancient Church of St Nicholas, the nearby Lynch's Castle and conserved Blake's Castle, combined with the Spanish Arch, the cathedral and the Nora Barnacle Museum are just some of Galway's visual treasures set to beguile the visitor. A step further in such beguilement is the Lynch Memorial Window, the world's first official tourist trap, commemorating an event that never really happened. But the native will still tell you how a fifteenth-century mayor hanged his son here, for Galway, both city and county, is a place where fact and fiction rest easy on the mind as well as in the telling.

SELECTED BIBLIOGRAPHY

Bourke, Eamonn, *Burke People and Places*, Castlebar, 1984.

Claffey, John A., *The Cathedral of the Assumption Tuam*, 1986.

Coen, Rev. Martin, *The Wardenship of Galway*, Galway, 1984.

Collins, Timothy, 'The Galway Line in Context: A Contribution to Galway Maritime History' in *JGAHS*, Vols 46, 47, 1994–5.

Dolan, M., 'Galway 1920–21' in *The Capucin Annual*, 1970.

Dutton, Hely, *A Statistical and Agricultural Survey of the County of Galway*, 1824.

Egan, Patrick K., *St. Brendan's Cathedral, Loughrea, Co. Galway*, The Irish Heritage Series, Dublin, 1986; *The Parish of Ballinasloe*, Galway, 1994.

Fahey, J., D.D., V.G., *The History and Antiquities of the Diocese of Kilmacduagh*, Dublin, 1893.

Fleetwood Berry, Rev. J., *The Story of St. Nicholas' Collegiate Church*, Galway, 1912, revised 1989.

Gosling, Paul, *Archaeological Inventory of County Galway*, Vol. 1, West Galway, Dublin, 1993, and Alcock, Olive, Gosling, Paul and de hÓra, Kathy, Vol. 11, North Galway, Dublin, 1999.

A Guide to Coole Park, Co. Galway Home of Lady Gregory, Colin Smythe, 1973.

Hall, Mr & Mrs S.C., *Ireland: Its Scenery, Character, Etc.*, London, 1842.

Hardiman, James, *History of the Town and County of Galway*, Dublin, 1820.

Henry, William, *The Shimmering Waste,* Galway, 1997; *Role of Honour: The Mayors of Galway City 1485–2001,* Galway, 2002.

Holland, P., 'The Anglo-Normans in Co. Galway' in *JGAHS,* Vol. 41, 1978–88; 'The Anglo-Normans and their Castles in Co. Galway' in Moran, G. and Gillespie, R.

Lalor, Brian, gen. ed., *The Encyclopaedia of Ireland,* Dublin, 2003.

Lawlor, Brendan and O'Dowd, Peadar, *Galway–Heart of the West,* Galway, 1991.

Kavanagh, Mary, *Galway–Gaillimh, A Bibliography of the City and County,* Galway, 2000.

Lynam, Joss, *The Mountains of Connemara: A Hill-Walker's Guide,* Roundstone, 1988.

May, Tom, *Churches of Galway, Kilmacduagh & Kilfenora,* Galway, 2000.

Melvin, Patrick, 'The Composition of the Galway Gentry' in *Clanricarde Country,* Woodford Heritage Group, 1987.

Mitchell, Dr James, 'Mayor Lynch of Galway: A Review of the Tradition' in *JGAHS,* Vol. 32, 1966–71.

Moran, Gerard and Gillespie, Raymond, eds, *Galway History & Society,* Dublin, 1996.

Murray, James P., *Galway: A Medico-Social History,* Galway.

Ó Cearbhaill, Diarmuid, ed., *Galway: Town & Gown 1484–1984,* Dublin, 1984.

O'Connor, Gabriel, *A History of Galway County Council,* Galway, 1999.

O'Dowd, Peadar, *Old & New Galway,* Galway, 1985; *Down by the Claddagh,* Galway, 1993; *Touring Galway–A Guide to County Galway, Ireland,* Galway, 1993; *The Great Famine and the West–1845–50,* Galway, 1996; *Galway City,* Galway, 1998; *In from the West–the McDonogh Dynasty,* Galway, 2002; *Galway City in Old Photographs,* Dublin, 2003.

O'Flaherty, Roderic (Hardiman, James, ed.), *A Choreographical Description of West or H-Iar Connaught,* Dublin, 1846.

Ó Laoí, Padraic, *Annals of the G.A.A. in Galway 1884–1901,* Galway, 1983.

O'Neill, T.P., *The Tribes and other Galway Families,* Galway, 1984.

O'Sullivan, M.D., *Old Galway–The History of a Norman Colony in Ireland,* Cambridge, 1942, reprinted in Galway, 1983.

Ó Tuathaigh, Gearóid, '. . . the air of a place of importance–Aspects of Nineteenth-Century Galway' in Ó Cearbhaill, D.

Robinson, Tim, *Connemara Part 1: Introduction and Gazetteer,* Roundstone, 1990; *Oileáin Árann, The Aran Islands, A Map and Guide,* Aran, 1980.

Rynne, Etienne, *Tourist Trail of Old Galway*, Galway, 1997; *Athenry A Medieval Irish Town*, Athenry, 1992.

Spellissy, Seán, *The History of Galway*, Limerick, 1999.

Townley, C., 'The Story of the Allan Shipping Line' in *Connacht Tribune*, 28 April 1967.

Villiers-Tuthill, Kathleen, *History of Clifden 1810–1860*, 1981.

Walsh, Paul, *Discover Galway*, Dublin, 2001.

Whitmarsh, Victor, *Shadows on Glass, Galway 1895–1960*, Galway, 2003.

Wilde, William, *Loch Coirib*, Dublin, 1867.

Woodford Heritage Group, *Clanricarde Country*, Woodford, 1987; Roche, Desmond and Shiel, Michael, *A Forgotten Campaign and Aspects of the Heritage of South East Galway*, Woodford, 1986.

Woodman, Kieran, Dr, *Safe and Commodious, The Annals of the Galway Harbour Commissioners, 1830–1997*, Galway, 2000; *Tribes to Tigers*, Galway, 2000.

I NDEX

Numbers in **bold** indicate an illustration.